Natural
Wonders
of
Virginia

Natural Wonders

of

Virginia

A Guide to Parks, Preserves & Wild Places

Garvey and Deane Winegar

Illustrated by Lois Leonard Stock

Country Roads Press

CASTINE • MAINE

Natural Wonders of Virginia

Published by Country Roads Press
P.O. Box 286, Lower Main Street
Castine, Maine 04421

Text and cover design by Studio 3.
Cover photograph by Deane Winegar.
Illustrations by Lois Leonard Stock.
Typesetting by Typeworks.

ISBN 1-56626-106-6

Library of Congress Cataloging-in-Publication Data

Winegar, Garvey.
    Natural wonders of Virginia : a guide to parks, preserves, and
wild places / Garvey and Deane Winegar ; illustrator: Lois Stock.
        p.   cm.
    Includes index.
    ISBN 1-56626-106-6 : $9.95
    1. Virginia — Guidebooks.   2. Natural history — Virginia —
Guidebooks.   3. Natural areas — Virginia — Guidebooks.
4. Parks — Virginia — Guidebooks.   5. Botanical gardens —
Virginia — Guidebooks.   I. Winegar, Deane.   II. Title.
F224.3.W56   1994
917.5504′43 — dc20   94-19186
                                                                          CIP

Printed in the United States of America.
10   9   8   7   6   5   4   3   2

To our Mothers,
Kitty Dozier and Mary Winegar,
who inspired us
to climb to the high places

Contents

Introduction   *xi*

1   MOUNTAIN REGION   *1*
Appalachian Trail   *1*
Blue Ridge Parkway, Skyline Drive, and
    Shenandoah National Park   *3*
Breaks Interstate Park   *15*
Caverns   *19*
Claytor Lake State Park   *20*
Cumberland Gap National Historical Park   *22*
Douthat State Park   *25*
Fairy Stone State Park   *27*
George Washington National Forest   *30*
Grayson Highlands State Park   *41*
Hungry Mother State Park   *45*
Jefferson National Forest   *47*
Lake Moomaw   *58*
Mount Rogers National Recreation Area   *62*
Natural Tunnel State Park   *66*

New River Trail State Park   *69*
Pinnacle Natural Area Preserve   *72*
Sky Meadows State Park   *74*
Smith Mountain Lake State Park   *78*
Virginia Creeper Trail   *80*

2 CENTRAL REGION (Piedmont)   *83*
Buggs Island Lake (Kerr Reservoir) and
     Lake Gaston   *83*
James River Park   *89*
Lake Anna State Park   *92*
Lake Parks of Central Piedmont   *95*
Lewis Ginter Botanical Garden   *98*
Maymont   *100*
Pocahontas State Park   *102*

3 TIDEWATER REGION   *107*
Back Bay National Wildlife Refuge and
     False Cape State Park   *107*
Caledon Natural Area   *112*
Chesapeake Bay   *115*
Chincoteague National Wildlife Refuge   *122*
Chippokes Plantation State Park   *128*
Great Dismal Swamp   *129*
Kiptopeke State Park   *134*
Leesylvania State Park   *138*
Mason Neck   *140*
Mount Vernon Trail   *143*
Norfolk Botanical Garden   *147*
Northern Virginia Regional Parks   *150*
Seashore State Park and Natural Area   *158*
Virginia Living Museum   *161*
Virginia Marine Science Museum   *163*
Virginia Zoological Park   *165*

Westmoreland State Park   167
York River State Park   169

4 CANOE TRAILS   **172**

Index   176

Introduction

The purpose of this book is simple: to share with you some of our favorite outdoor places in Virginia.

Featured in these pages are mountains where the raven soars over alpine meadows, and spring-fed streams where native trout dart beneath the shadows of giant hemlocks.

We'll visit parks with lakes and campgrounds and twilight programs. We'll also travel to beaches where you can pitch a tent or take a walk with the pounding surf of the Atlantic as company. There are destinations to attract families, with swimming pools and playgrounds surrounded by natural loveliness, where the happy sounds of children at play quite likely override the cry of passing wild geese.

There are also deep forests and remote wilderness areas of inestimable beauty where you can find solitude.

Not included are a few of the most fragile wild places, such as the holdings of The Nature Conservancy and the natural areas of the Department of Conservation and Recreation. Until public access is invited and trails are constructed in a way to protect at-risk soil, sand dunes, wildflowers, or wetlands, it's best that we all leave these areas to the flora and fauna nurtured there. No one wants to see in wilderness the same eroded ruts that relentless foot traffic has carved into the popular Appalachian Trail.

Some things will actually be improved by the time you arrive. Recently, Virginia residents approved a $95 million bond for renovation and construction at the state's aging parks as well as its relatively new natural areas. Expect to see work begun or completed on new facilities. Hiking trails are being cleared, bathhouses and cabins modernized, campgrounds upgraded.

Individual maps are available for lakes, rivers, and parks across the state. A good source is Alexandria Drafting Company, 6440 General Green Way, Alexandria, VA 22312 (800-ADC-MAPS).

Topographic maps, preferred by hikers and canoeists for their detail, are published by the U.S. Geological Survey. For a guide that shows what maps are available across the state, contact the Virginia Division of Mineral Resources, P.O. Box 3667, McCormick Road, Charlottesville, VA 22903 (804-293-5121).

For a packet of information on specific areas of the state that interest you, contact the Virginia Division of Tourism, Bell Tower, Capitol Grounds, P.O. Box 798, Richmond, VA 23219 (804-786-4484).

Because state campgrounds and cabins are located in some of the most beautiful and interesting parts of Virginia, they fill up early. We recommend reservations (800-933-PARK).

For a free color brochure or more information on individual parks, contact the Virginia Department of Conservation and Recreation, 203 Governor Street, Richmond, VA 23219 (804-786-1712).

For fishing and hunting licenses and other information, contact the Department of Game and Inland Fisheries, 4010 West Broad Street, Richmond, VA 23230 (804-367-1000).

To help clarify road designations, we've used the following abbreviations: I=interstate, US=U.S. route or highway,

State = state route or highway, and County = county road. We're indebted to the Virginia Department of Conservation and Recreation and especially Gary Waugh, communications manager, for generous help. Waugh pointed out several interesting features in state parks and natural areas that we might not have discovered on our own. A special thanks also to W. Terry Smith, public affairs officer with the George Washington National Forest, Donna Wilson, public affairs specialist with the Jefferson National Forest, and the many others who offered help and suggestions along the way.

As you will learn, Virginia's natural wonders are so diverse, they could be located in three—maybe four—different countries rather than a single state. The mile-high mountains of the far southwest represent a world distinct from the sea-level beaches of Chesapeake Bay or the urban congestion of northern Virginia near Washington, D.C. Mores, culture, even speech, are different.

Now it's time to travel. A note for teachers: Eight Chesapeake Bay parks participate in the program "Virginia's State Parks: Your Backyard Classrooms." A forty-activity curriculum guide is available for teachers of grades K-12. Participating parks are Caledon Natural Area, Chippokes Plantation State Park, Kiptopeke State Park, Leesylvania State Park, Mason Neck State Park, Seashore State Park, Westmoreland State Park, and York River State Park. For more information, call 804-786-1712. We were very lucky to be able to crisscross Virginia several times while researching this book. Go and do likewise.

1

Mountain Region

APPALACHIAN TRAIL

More than one-fourth of the famous 2,000-mile-long Appalachian Trail, which extends from Georgia to Maine, winds through Virginia. Although fourteen states claim a part of this white-blazed path along the backbone of the eastern seaboard, no other state comes anywhere near the 545 miles of trail in the Old Dominion.

The little town of Damascus, Virginia, which has earned the name "Friendliest Town on the Appalachian Trail" for its hospitality, welcomes Appalachian Trail hikers into Virginia from the south. After an invigorating—and rewarding—54.6 miles through Mount Rogers National Recreation Area, hikers follow a serpentine path through Jefferson National Forest.

At Roanoke, the trail heads east across the Great Valley to connect with the Blue Ridge Mountains. Then it's north to Rockfish Gap and into Shenandoah National Park. The well-cared-for park portion of the trail is noted for its challenging up-and-down terrain.

Despite the fact that the Appalachian Trail is an unbroken link from Georgia to Maine—an automatic challenge to some to tackle the whole length at one stretch—the vast majority of hikers take on small pieces of it at any one time. Most people who hike the entire length of the trail start from Georgia in early spring and hike north to finish in Maine in the fall. White blazes mark the trail proper, with spur and access trails marked with blue. Two blazes, one above the other, warn of a change in route ahead. Marks are usually no more than a quarter mile apart.

If you hike portions of the Appalachian Trail frequently, you may wonder who dragged off the scrub pine that fell across the trail in Big Meadows, and who was responsible for that sturdy log footbridge that kept your feet dry as you crossed Fox Creek in Mount Rogers National Recreaton Area. It was probably a hodgepodge of trail clubs, volunteers, state and federal agencies, and even conscientious hikers who all pitch in to maintain this scenic and historic footpath. Coordinating much of the work is the devoted Appalachian Trail Conference, with energetic member chapters supplying muscle power all along the route.

Shelters and lean-tos for overnighters are well spaced along the trail. If these are already occupied when you arrive, it's all right to camp nearby at a respectable distance.

Where: Enters Virginia about four miles south of Damascus, follows mountains northeast to Harper's Ferry, WV.
Hours: Always open.
Admission: No fee.
Best time to visit: Anytime.
Activities: Hiking, nature and wildlife observation, primitive camping.
Concessions: None on trail itself.
Pets: Dogs under owner's control permitted. Must be leashed in Shenandoah National Park

Other: Side trails to beautiful waterfalls, especially in Shenandoah National Park. (One closest to trail is Dark Hollow Falls at Big Meadows.)

For more information:

National Office, Appalachian Trail Conference, P.O. Box 807, Harpers Ferry, WV 25425 (304-535-6331).

Charles Graf, President, Potomac Appalachian Trail Club, 118 Park Street SE, Vienna, VA 22180-4609 (410-757-6053).

Theresa Duffey, President, Old Dominion Appalachian Trail Club, 6220 Club Road, Richmond, VA 23228 [804-266-7913 (home) or 804-786-5053 (work)].

Mike Brewer, President, Tidewater Appalachian Trail Club, 138 Wythe Parkway, Hampton, VA 23661 [804-247-1895 (home) or 804-727-6548 (work)].

Michael McCormack, President, Natural Bridge Appalachian Trail Club, P.O. Box 497, Amherst, VA 24521 [804-384-1944 (home) or 804-947-2159 (work)].

Hal Cantrill, President, Roanoke Appalachian Trail Club, 208 Eagle Drive, Salem, VA 24153 [703-387-2347 (home) or 703-387-7319 (work)].

Jenny Golding, President, Outing Club of Virginia Tech, P.O. Box 538, Blacksburg, VA 24060.

Michael Diflora, President, Mount Rogers Appalachian Trail Club, 153 Kingsbridge, Bristol, VA 37620 [615-652-7695 (home) or 703-466-4121 (work)].

BLUE RIDGE PARKWAY, SKYLINE DRIVE, AND SHENANDOAH NATIONAL PARK

Skyline Drive and the Blue Ridge Parkway — Virginia's two end-to-end highways in the clouds — offer an unusual perspective on the Old Dominion. Charles Kuralt says the mountaintop drive is one of the ten most beautiful drives in America.

Whereas museums attempt to preserve what man has done, these two highways – especially Skyline Drive – lead you through remote mountains where man's influence is slowly being allowed to fade with the passing of time.

Take Shenandoah National Park, which straddles the Blue Ridge Mountains for 105 scenic miles from Front Royal (mile 0) to Rockfish Gap near Waynesboro (mile 105). Skyline Drive runs the ridge crest for the length of the park. Stop at an overlook and enjoy one of the hiking trails in the national park – including a ninety-five-mile section of the Appalachian Trail – and you'll see that the Blue Ridge range is being allowed to revert to true wilderness.

Today, Shenandoah National Park looks much as it did when Monocan and Monahoac Native Americans inhabited the area centuries before the first white settlers stepped ashore at Jamestown. Gone are the hardscrabble farms whose thin soil washed away with every rain. Gone are the vast clearings where early white settlers overharvested timber from the high ridges. Native Americans, too, burned large areas in order to drive game within range of their Stone Age weapons.

The park today is 300 square miles of gentle wilderness, of native trout streams and waterfalls and wildflowers, of black bear and white-tailed deer. Less than 4 percent of the Park is developed, and that 4 percent runs along the Skyline Drive.

Most people use the words "Skyline Drive" and "Blue Ridge Parkway" interchangeably. It's a mistake, but not a serious one. Both mountain highways are federal roads, two-lane and gently serpentine, with some of the most spectacular scenery in the East. The southern end of Skyline Drive and the northern end of the Blue Ridge Parkway join at Rockfish Gap near Waynesboro, but you'd never know when you leave one and pick up the other if signs didn't alert you.

The Blue Ridge Parkway is by far the longest of these two remarkable highways. The parkway threads along the crest of the Blue Ridge Mountains from Rockfish Gap (mile 0) south to the Great Smoky Mountains National Park in North Carolina (mile 469).

Both highways were built for scenic value and not speed. Top legal speed is 45 mph on the parkway and 35 mph on Skyline Drive. A common mistake for travelers is to bite off more than they really want to chew. A hundred miles or so is enough in one stint on either highway. By then you'll be ready for less winding and mountainous driving and may actually welcome the interstate system again. Strategically placed exits on both scenic roads make it easy to get on and off. Restaurants, gas stations, scenic overlooks, campgrounds, and overnight lodges are spaced along the length of both highways.

Generations of mountain people lived off the land in the area now embraced by Shenandoah National Park, Skyline Drive, and the Blue Ridge Parkway. The National Park Service has preserved examples of the culture of these hardy pioneers at a number of visitors centers.

For example, at Humpback Rocks (mile 5.8 to mile 9.3 on the parkway), a reconstructed mountain farm homestead with many of the crude, handmade tools used by mountaineers is open to visitors.

At Mabry Mill (mile 176.1), there's a picturesque water-powered gristmill and blacksmith shop, both in operation.

And at Byrd Visitor Center at Big Meadows on Skyline Drive near Luray, some of the vast meadows that have been in existence since before Columbus are kept open for wildflowers and as places to watch deer in the evenings.

Here is a more complete list of concessions, campgrounds, and attractions along these roads:

Skyline Drive, North to South

Campgrounds have drinking water, comfort stations, and showers, but no utility connections.

Mile 4.6, Dickey Ridge Visitor Center – Major information facility with publications and maps, self-guiding trail.

Mile 24.1, Elkwallow Gap – Food service, camp store, gas, souvenirs.

Mile 31.5, Thornton Gap – Panorama Restaurant, gift shop.

Mile 41.7 and 42.5, Skyland – Primary tourist stop with lodge, dining room, gift shop, riding horses, guided hikes, interpretive programs, Stony Man Nature Trail.

Mile 51 and 51.2, Big Meadows – Major information facility with Byrd Visitor Center, publications and maps, ranger programs, self-guiding nature trail, campground, cabins, coffee shop, camp store, two gift shops, service station, lodge with dining room.

Mile 57.5, Lewis Mountain – Cabins, campground, camp store, campfire programs.

Mile 79.5, Loft Mountain – Campground, camp store, gift shop, showers, laundry, self-guiding nature trail, conducted hikes, campfire programs in summer.

Blue Ridge Parkway, North to South

Campgrounds have drinking water and comfort stations but no showers or utility connections.

Mile 5.8 to 9.3, Humpback Rocks – Visitors center, self-guiding trail, hiking, Pioneer Village exhibit.

Mile 29, Whetstone Ridge – Restaurant, gas.

Mile 58 to 63.6, Otter Creek – Campground, restaurant, gas, fishing, trail, James River and Kanawha Canal exhibit and restored canal lock, self-guiding trail.

Mile 84 to 87, Peaks of Otter – Popular destination point with restaurant, lodge, and rooms with a lake view, visitors center, gas, campgrounds, shuttle bus to panoramic view at peak, trails.

Mile 167 to 174, Rocky Knob – Campground, hiking trails, housekeeping cabins.

Mile 176.1, Mabry Mill – Sawmill, blacksmith shop, gristmill, restaurant.

A white-tailed buck

WHITE-TAILED DEER

The Virginia white-tailed deer is one of the shining success stories of game management. There are far more deer in the state today than when early settlers hunted the animal for its hide and meat. Through the restoration of habitat and regulation of hunting, the deer population has climbed from a low of next to nothing at the turn of the century to an estimated one million animals today.

The health of the deer herd can only be good news for those who walk forest paths and love to come upon the graceful animal. On summer evenings, you find deer searchers (including ourselves) driving the byways and back roads, scanning the far edges of hazy fields, saying, "There—up close against the woods! Is that one?"

Big Meadows in Shenandoah National Park is the classic destination for deer searchers. Bring binoculars. Deer aren't particularly skittish here, but they'll move off if you try to get too close. Hunting is outlawed in the park, and the deer have learned they have nothing to fear from people. At dusk, they come out of the woods from all sides and into the wide expanse of cranberry bog and open fields that give Big Meadows its name. The deer browse here throughout the night. If you crawl out of your tent or camping trailer early enough, you can watch the morning sun glow red off their coats before they depart ghostlike into the shadows.

During the fall mating season, big bucks throw all caution to the wind and follow—or harass—does into Big Meadows even at midday.

If you don't see deer in the open fields or grazing along the roadside, you'll usually see a few along the nature trail and path connecting the campground to the visitors center. From June through the fall, look for the engaging white-spotted fawns sticking close to the does.

Bucks often stay together, apart from the does, until mating season, when they part company with other males and compete for the available females. Each year bucks develop new antlers, which grow under a velvet-covered supply of blood vessels all summer. In fall, the velvet is rubbed off (look for the telltale scraped bark of saplings), revealing the new set of antlers, varying from small spikes in young or stunted animals to massive, spreading racks in larger, healthier males.

The Appalachian Trail

For most of its length, Skyline Drive plays a close game of tag with the famous Appalachian Trail, which extends from northern Georgia to Maine. If you're hiking the Trail, you'll be less aware of the sounds of vehicles from the Blue Ridge Parkway. The Appalachian Trail roughly parallels the parkway from mile zero at Afton Mountain to mile 103 just north of Roanoke, where the trail and the parkway separate for the rest of the Virginia stretch.

There are many other hiking trails off Skyline Drive and the Blue Ridge Parkway. In Shenandoah National Park alone are more than 500 miles of trails. Some of our favorites are those that go to waterfalls. At mile 50.7 on Skyline Drive near Big Meadows Lodge is Dark Hollow Falls, the cascade closest to the road and perhaps the most visited. It's a steep climb down to view the seventy-foot falls, but the entire round-trip is only 1.5 miles. Park personnel and literature can direct you to other waterfall trails.

At Elkwallow Gap (mile 24.1), a major detour to the Appalachian Trail takes off to meet with the Alleghenies to the west. Called the Big Blue for its blue blazes, the trail then heads north into Pennsylvania, where it becomes the Tuscarora Trail and eventually rejoins the Appalachian Trail.

On the Blue Ridge Parkway, the three-quarter-mile hike from the parking area at mile 6.1 to Humpback Rocks takes you to a spectacular view of the Shenandoah Valley. If the fairly steep climb doesn't take your breath away, the scenery will.

For a greater challenge, climb the winding trail to the huge boulders of Sharptop at Peaks of Otter (mile 86) for a full-circle view of valleys and mountains. Don't be surprised to find people at the top who've ridden the shuttle bus, for there's a paved road all the way up. If you hiked, you'll arrive back at the Peaks of Otter Lodge hungry for the outstanding buffet.

Where: Skyline Drive and Shenandoah National Park run along crest of Blue Ridge from Front Royal south to Waynesboro. Blue

HAWK-WATCHING

On the cool winds of autumn they come, following unmarked and ancient avian highways along Virginia's mountain ranges, Piedmont section, and even down the shores of Chesapeake Bay.

For hawks and other birds of prey, September is a major travel month. Hundreds of thousands of these migrators funnel through Virginia as they head south for the winter. While we scrape ice in February, they bask in the tropical warmth of Mexico and Central and South America. Some of the raptors travel as far as Peru and Argentina.

If you own or can borrow a pair of binoculars, you have all the equipment you need to join the hawk-watchers on the Blue Ridge Parkway for the annual fall migration. Many observers log long hours, sitting in folding chairs at overlooks to identify different migrating species and compare the numbers from year to year. The results are tabulated by the Hawk Migration Association of North America.

Birds counted include the red-tailed hawk, broad-winged hawk, red-shouldered hawk, bald eagle, osprey, peregrine falcon, kestrel, Cooper's hawk, sharp-shinned hawk, and northern harrier.

Favored lookout points are usually located on the crest of long, narrow ridges with abrupt slopes. During the peak season you can almost always find knowledgeable folks eager to help others learn to identify the birds. You might see a few raptors or you might get lucky and see "kettles" of several hundred at a time, depending on conditions. One such place of abundance is at Rockfish Gap on Afton Mountain near Waynesboro, where the Blue Ridge Parkway and Skyline Drive meet. Observers use an overlook adjacent to the Holiday Inn. One unforgettable September day, they recorded an astounding 10,596 raptors. Contact YuLee Larner, 1020 West Beverley street, Staunton, VA 24401 (703-886-7815).

Another spot is the Harvey's Knob overlook on the Blue Ridge Parkway, approximately fifteen miles northeast of Roanoke. Contact David J. Holt, 3094 Forest Acre Trail, Salem, VA 24153 (703-384-6674).

To learn more about the Hawk Migration Association, write Robert E. Lindsay, 19977 Wild Cherry Lane, Germantown, MD 20874.

A red-tailed hawk

Ridge Parkway starts at Waynesboro and runs south along ridge crest to Great Smoky Mountains in North Carolina, exiting Virginia at mile 216.9.

Hours: Parkway open all year, weather permitting. Skyline Drive sometimes closes at night during fall deer hunting season to discourage poaching. Neither road plowed when it snows. Most facilities open spring through fall. Big Meadows campground, lodge, and wayside usually closed from November through March. Peaks of Otter Lodge and Restaurant on Blue Ridge Parkway open all year. Reservations for camping and lodging may be necessary summer through fall.

Admission: No fee for parkway; entrance fee for Skyline Drive and park. Campground fees.

Best time to visit: Early May for flowering dogwood, late May and June for rhododendron, mountain laurel; mid-October for fall foliage (weekdays less crowded); winter for cross-country skiing.

Activities: Scenic drives, hiking, bicycling, cross-country skiing, camping, wildlife observation, picnicking.

Pets: Must be on leash on Blue Ridge Parkway and Skyline Drive.

Points of Interest

Museum of American Frontier Culture, Staunton — For an interesting side trip, visit this living history exhibit of authentic working farms of the eighteenth and nineteenth centuries, about twenty minutes west of Rockfish Gap, where the Blue Ridge Parkway meets Skyline Drive. You will see not only an American farm, but actual farm buildings from Germany, Ireland, and England that strongly influenced early life in the United States. Special events held throughout the year include a cornhusking bee, threshing party, and Guy Fawkes Day celebration. The museum is open daily 10:00 A.M. to 4:00 P.M. December 1 to March 15 and 9:00 A.M. to 5:00 P.M. March 16 to November 30.

From Waynesboro, take I-64 west to I-81 north. Stay in the right lane for exit 222 to US 250 west, then follow the signs to the museum.

Wintergreen Resort, Wintergreen — Here in the mountains is food for both body and soul. Just a mile east of Blue Ridge

Parkway milepost 13.5 on steep County 664 is the upper entrance to this 11,000-acre resort, with its strong outdoor program and miles of scenic blazed hiking trails, varying in difficulty and length. Take a lunch break at one of Wintergreen's several restaurants, or, if you arrive on a Sunday, follow the tantalizing aromas to the Coppermine Restaurant's opulent smorgasbord, politely called the Sunday Brunch.

Then stop at the Outdoor Center in the resort's Mountain Village for trail maps. The staff will have tips about what wildflowers are blooming and where they've seen a fawn hiding in tall grass or a gray fox dashing across the path. Look up Doug Coleman, Wintergreen's naturalist, who has been instrumental in keeping the resort's award-winning environmental program on track.

Several trails access different parts of Big Stony Run, which rushes between banks lined with hemlock and ferns down one of the deepest gorges in the eastern United States. At the headwaters is Shamokin Springs Nature Preserve, where you might photograph such wildflowers as speckled wood lily, wild lily-of-the-valley, spotted coralroot orchid, monkshood, and turk's-cap lily.

Along the Upper Shamokin Gorge Trail, which leads to the Upper Shamokin Falls on Big Stony, we have found the delicate white petals of bloodroot, pink lady's slipper, and several varieties of trillium poking through the dead leaves in spring.

You can also hike from the valley up to the dramatic lower falls, which cascades between boulders from 100 feet above to form a hollowed-out pool big enough for cooling off. On the streambank, look for the secretive jack-in-the-pulpit emerging in the damp soil between the sturdy roots of a white oak or tulip poplar.

In mid-May, at the height of the trillium bloom and peak of the spring wildflower season, Wintergreen hosts an outstanding wildflower symposium. Botanists, ornithologists, and other experts from across the country lead wildflower and birding walks and conduct workshops on such subjects as cooking with edible wild plants, wildflower photography, woodland salamanders, and propagating native plants. Reservations are required.

Mill Mountain Zoo, Roanoke — Located just three miles from the Blue Ridge Parkway at Roanoke, the ten-acre Mill Mountain Zoo is open daily 10:00 A.M. to 6:00 P.M. and exhibits forty-five species of exotic and native animals in a scenic mountaintop setting. On winding, wooded trails just outside the zoo entrance is a garden of propagated wildflowers established by a local horticultural society. To reach the zoo and garden, take the parkway spur road at mile 120.3, go three miles, and follow the signs.

For more information:

Shenandoah National Park, Park Service Headquarters, Route 4, Box 348, Luray, VA 22835 (703-999-2243). For general information, call 703-999-2266. For information on lodging and other services, contact park concessionaire ARA Virginia Sky-Line Co., Inc., P.O. Box 727NP, Luray, VA 22835 (800-999-4714). For maps, pamphlets, trail guides, et cetera, contact the nonprofit Shenandoah Natural History Association, Route 4, Box 348, Luray, VA 22835 (703-999-3582).

Blue Ridge Parkway, National Park Service, 200 B B and T Building, Asheville, NC 28801 (704-298-0398).

Museum of American Frontier Culture, P.O. Box 810, Staunton, VA 24402 (703-332-7850).

Peaks of Otter Lodge, P.O. Box 489, Bedford, VA 24523 (703-586-1081).

Mill Mountain Zoo, Blue Ridge Zoological Society of Virginia, P.O. Box 13484, Roanoke, VA 24034 (703-343-3241).

Wintergreen Outdoor Center, P.O. Box 706, Wintergreen, VA 22958 (804-325-2200).

BREAKS INTERSTATE PARK

Hallowed ground. That's how the native Cherokee thought of this stunning five-mile-long pass through the Cumberland Mountains. The Cherokee believed these mountains, this raging river, this deep and spectacular gorge to be blessed.

Actually, if you've a pantheistic bone in your body, or if there are Druids in your distant past, it's tempting to stand on the canyon rim of Breaks Interstate Park in Dickenson County and cock an ear.

On a windy, cold day when soiled patches of snow and ice clung to the coal-blackened walls of State 80 leading from Haysi to the park, we stood at the rim of this canyon a quarter mile above the cascading Russell Fork of the Big Sandy River as it roared through Breaks park. But we heard no voices and saw no visions. We received no heavenly clues regarding the stock market, our love life, or the state lottery. Just the same, the visit wasn't what you'd call wasted.

The promoters like to refer to Breaks Interstate Park as the "Grand Canyon of the South." We like better the "Grand Canyon with clothes on," which alludes to the forested canyon walls and the spectacular scenery extending into Tennessee and Kentucky.

Of course, this isn't the Grand Canyon, but it'll do. The Russell Fork River through Breaks Interstate Park has, over some 250 million years, gouged out the longest and deepest canyon east of the Mississippi.

The sheer vertical walls fall away a thousand feet at several park overlooks, and the sound of the river drifting up from below is an unceasing distant roar.

Mature rhododendron blankets the mountain slopes. This is an incredibly beautiful place in May and June when the pink and purple flowers are in bloom. This particular morning, however, the waxy green leaves of the rhododendron are drooped and curled in upon themselves. Rhododendron leaves do that when the temperature drops below twenty-eight degrees.

Since frontier times, the Cumberland Mountains have been a barrier to westward migration. Early setters located gaps, or "breaks," in the 125-mile-long Cumberland range. The most famous is Cumberland Gap, 100 miles to the southwest. When roads were being built into this area during the Depression, local people referred to the gap which gave the park its name simply as "The Breaks."

Virginia and Kentucky share Breaks Interstate Park. The joint 4,600-acre park opened with just 100 acres in 1957. Most of the park is in rural Dickenson County, which is one of the few counties in Virginia that does not have a U.S. highway within its borders.

This area is close to the heart of the Virginia coalfields. People who live here are nearer Cincinnati than their state capital. Roads are winding and two-lane. Houses and trailers perch on hillsides for the simple reason that if you choose to live in these vast mountains, there's precious little flat land to go around.

As late as World War II, few outsiders had visited The Breaks. In 1900, John Fox Jr., author of *The Trail of the Lonesome Pine*, generated the first widespread interest in this remote country when he traveled three days by horse-drawn buckboard from Big Stone Gap, seventy miles distant, and wrote about his trip in *Scribner's* magazine. He called The Breaks the "most isolated spot this side of the Rockies."

We've made this trip to the park during the off-season. The Rhododendron Restaurant — well known for its cuisine — seems to hang out over the canyon, but it's closed for the season. The swimming pool is iced over and the campground is closed.

Several contemporary, fully equipped two-bedroom cottages are open at the park throughout the year, rented at reasonable prices. But they are available only on a weekly basis.

There's an attractive motor lodge at the park, with stunning views from the balcony of each of the thirty-four rooms, but it too is closed.

So we stay in Breaks Motor Lodge, a modest mom-and-pop motel two miles from the park entrance on the road to Elkhorn City, Kentucky. The motel has sulfur water, which certainly spices up a shower.

Old-time gospel sings are held at The Breaks on certain summer weekends. They attract several thousand visitors, but the first one won't roll around until Memorial Day weekend.

There's trout fishing in the river, and two lakes in the park are stocked with bass and bluegill. But it's too cold to fish.

Until recent years, Dickenson County was one of two counties closed to deer hunting in Virginia because of a scarcity of deer. The mountains have been restocked with deer, however, resulting in a return of the whitetail. We saw the sharp V-shaped hoofprint where deer had crossed the hiking trail.

Nearby in Dickenson County is the John W. Flannagan Reservoir, a deep, 1,143-acre lake with a steep shoreline. Built by the U.S. Army Corps of Engineers as a flood-control lake on the Pound River, Flannagan holds catfish, largemouth bass, spotted bass, sunfish, and walleye, and is probably underfished.

Eight whitewater rafting outfitters take people down the class IV rapids of the Russell Fork on October weekends when enough water is released from John Flannagan Dam. You may bring your own canoes or kayaks. Rafting companies that run the fork are: Russell Fork Whitewater Adventures (703-530-7243), Elkhorn City Rafting Company (606-754-8274), USA Whitewater, Inc. (800-USA-RAFT), Cherokee Adventures (800-445-7238), Precision Rafting Expeditions (800-PRE-RAFT), Laurel Highlands River Tours, Inc. (800-4-RAFTIN), Wahoo's Adventures (800-444-RAFT), and Whitewater Adventures (800-WWA-RAFT).

There are twelve miles of hiking trails throughout the park.

Some trails are easy, some moderately difficult. Others are downright demanding, according to the park brochure. Yes, one look at this canyon shows how that might be.

So on this trip we'll walk the ridges and hollows the Native Americans held sacred, and try to remain open to guidance of one sort or another.

Where: At northern tip of Dickenson County in southwestern Virginia, near Kentucky state line. From Haysi, take State 80 to the park, on left.

Hours: Hiking and fishing, dawn to dusk, year-round. House-keeping cottages, weekly basis, year-round. Restaurant (7:00 A.M. to 9:00 P.M.), motor lodge, visitors center, campground (first come, first served), daily April 1 to October 31. Pool, interpretive program, horseback riding (10:00 A.M. to 6:00 P.M.), Memorial Day weekend to Labor Day.

Admission: Small parking fee; modest pool fee, campsite fees; paddleboat fee, horse and pony rental fee.

Best time to visit: Anytime for hiking, picnicking, scenery (roads can be impassable in winter). Spring for wildflowers, budding and flowering trees. Summer for relief from city traffic and heat. Labor Day weekend for Gospel Sing. Fall for scenery.

Activities: Scenic vistas, hiking trails (including two self-guiding trails), picnicking (shelters available), swimming in Olympic-sized pool, fishing for bass and bluegill and boating (no gasoline motors) on twelve-acre Laurel Lake, whitewater boating (rafting trips available in October), horseback riding, shaded campsites (some with electric, water, sewer), children's equipped play areas, housekeeping cottages, interpretive program, amphitheater, visitors center.

Concessions: Restaurant, gift shop, pool, snack bar, whitewater rafting.

Pets: Must be on leash.

Other: Memorial Day Gospel Sing (Sunday), Father's Day Gospel Sing, Labor Day weekend Tri-State Gospel Sing, mid-

September arts and crafts festival, mid-October Fall Foliage Festival.

For more information:

Breaks Interstate Park, PO Box 100, Breaks, VA 24607-0100 (703-865-4413 or 804-786-1712). For motor lodge reservations, call 800-982-5122.

For details on either hunting or fishing, contact the Virginia Department of Game and Inland Fisheries, 4010 West Broad Street, Richmond, VA 23230-1104 (804-367-1000).

CAVERNS

Virginia's 3,000 caves vary in size from cramped crawlways to upward of twenty miles of interconnected passages with rooms large enough for dancing the Virginia reel. More than 95 percent are on private property. Visitors are charged a modest fee.

Caves and caverns show stunning evidence of the power of water to erode, change, and shape underground rock over millions of years. Caves are also home to various critters, but man is the largest visitor.

Eight species of bats are found in the state's caves. Three of the bat species—the Indiana bat, the gray bat and the Virginia big-eared bat—are on the federal endangered species list.

Cudjos Caverns, Cumberland Gap National Historical Park, about 800 feet east of the Virginia-Tennessee state line and east of Middlesboro, Kentucky, on US 25E (703-861-2203).

Dixie Caverns, towering chamber, drapery formations, exit 132 off I-81 or seven miles west of Salem on US 11 (703-380-2085).

Grand Caverns, one of the largest cavern rooms in the eastern U.S., just south of Grottoes off US 340 at Grand Caverns Regional Park (702-249-5705 or 703-249-5729).

Endless Caverns, giant columns and stone shields, three

miles south of New Market on US 11 (800-544-CAVE, 703-740-3993 or 703-896-2283).

Luray Caverns, unusual organ uses stalactites to make music; car and carriage museum, US 211, West Main Street in Luray (703-743-6551).

Massanutten Caverns, colorful rock formations, 0.5 mile northeast of Keezletown and six miles southeast of Harrisonburg via US 33 and State 620 (703-269-6555).

Caverns of Natural Bridge, underground streams, waterfalls, catacombs, US 11 near Natural Bridge, between I-81 exits 175 and 180 (703-291-2121). At nearby Natural Bridge, 215-foot-high arch spans creek, supports US 11.

Shenandoah Caverns, Oriental garden, elevators in caverns, I-81 exit 269 north of New Market, north on State 730 (703-477-3115).

Skyline Caverns, flowerlike formations, three underground streams, one mile south of Front Royal on US 340 (703-635-4545).

For more information:

Virginia Cave Board, Department of Conservation and Recreation, 203 Governor Street, Suite 302, Richmond, VA 23219 (804-786-1712).

CLAYTOR LAKE STATE PARK

Sprawling Claytor Lake, the focal point of Claytor Lake State Park, is deep, cold, clear, and twenty-one miles long—big enough to support a sizable population of various game fish, and with plenty of room to take a long and leisurely boat cruise.

The lake has smallmouth bass, walleye, and striped bass, all of which prefer the relatively unspoiled, oxygen-rich water of the New River, which was impounded to form the lake.

In fact, for many years Claytor held the Virginia state record for smallmouth bass. Even today, Claytor Lake and New River remain a source of some of the state's best smallmouth bass fishing. White bass are also plentiful. The Virginia Department of Game and Inland Fisheries annually stocks striped bass and walleye. Flathead catfish, channel catfish, crappie, and sunfish also keep anglers occupied.

The 472-acre park is located in a bend of the lake southeast of Dublin. It has a full-service marina with rental boat slips, rental rowboats, gas, bait, tackle, and snack food.

If fishing doesn't interest you, take a cruise in the elegant *Pioneer Maid* around this power-company impoundment. Spring through fall, the popular cruise boat transports passengers around the 4,475-acre lake.

Pick your spot early on the sandy swimming beach. There are few other places to swim on this big lake. On sweltering July weekends, this lifeguarded beach is in big demand.

On a cool morning, taking the Shady Ridge Nature Trail is a pleasant way to start the day. Pick up the guide booklet for the trail at the visitors center in the historic Howe House, built in the nineteenth century.

Twelve fully furnished housekeeping cabins are located at water's edge, and 132 campsites, 44 with hookups, are situated among the trees.

Where: Southeast of Dublin in southwestern Virginia. From I-81, take exit 101 and follow signs.
Hours: 8:00 a.m until dusk daily, year-round. Campgrounds open spring through fall (dates vary from year to year).
Admission: Small parking fee. Fee for camping, cabin rental, swimming, lake cruises, boat launching.
Best time to visit: Spring through fall for camping, fishing, boating. Summer for swimming. Anytime for hiking. (Weekends and holidays may be crowded.)

Activities: Boating (motorboats permitted), boat launching (on lake, on New River, and on State 100 at Goose Creek and Peak Creek), fishing, swimming, picnicking (shelter available), camping, housekeeping cabins, hiking, self-guiding trails, playground, amphitheater, interpretive programs, visitors center, cruise boat. *Concessions:* Marina, cruise boat, rowboat rental, rental boat slips, snack bar.
Pets: Must be on leash.
Other: Virginia Mountain Crafts Guild annual arts and crafts festival, Labor Day weekend.
For more information:

   Claytor Lake State Park, Route 1, Box 267, Dublin, VA 24084 (703-674-5492 or 804-786-1712).

CUMBERLAND GAP NATIONAL HISTORICAL PARK

Like Moses's famous mountaintop, this place once provided a vista to the promised land.

   Not only can you stand on Pinnacle Overlook and see into three states (Virginia, Tennessee, and Kentucky), but from here you can follow an important progression in United States history. With imagination, you may even be able to glance back several hundred years.

   The fabled Cumberland Gap is connected forever in legend and song to Daniel Boone, who led trudging pioneers through this narrow V in the sandstone and limestone wall of the Appalachian Mountains. From here settlers spread out to Kentucky, Ohio, and beyond the Mississippi.

   Cumberland Gap National Historical Park is a place for quiet contemplation. If your interests run to history and the expansion of empire rather than ski lifts and water slides, the park was created with you in mind.

   Pick up a brochure at the visitors center. Then drive through an arbor of overhanging boughs up the steep road that leads to the parking lot at the pinnacle. Unless your car has a hinge in the middle, don't expect to make much speed. The road is so narrow and curvy that it practically meets itself several times. Vehicles over 20 feet long are prohibited.

From the upper parking lot, the hardtop path leads 200 yards to Pinnacle Overlook. Look for the white line in the path. On one side of the line is Kentucky; on the other, Virginia. Tennessee is due south.

The view across three states is majestic. Mountains march off in all directions as far as the eye can see. On days when the air is clear of haze, peaks almost 100 miles distant shimmer on the horizon.

At the top, remains of Civil War fortifications are still visible. On some of the large boulders are the carved initials of soldiers who camped in the pass, or died trying to hold it. Union soldiers came pouring through this gap to invade Tennessee in 1862 and 1863.

Two vehicular tunnels, each nearly a mile in length, are being drilled through the solid rock of the mountain. When cars and trucks begin to use the tunnels, modern travelers will go beneath rather than over Cumberland Gap. The gap will then be restored to resemble what it used to be—the Warrior's Path for the Native Americans and the Wilderness Trail for settlers and adventurers from the American colonies on the East Coast.

Millions of buffalo and deer, Native American raiding and hunting parties, white settlers, soldiers, and tourists have used the narrow pass to get from one side of the imposing Appalachian range to the other. From the overlook, you can hike the Ridge Trail north about nine miles to the Hensley settlement on Brush Mountain. There you can see the restored hand-hewn log buildings with shake roofs that remain from twelve farmsteads constructed in the early 1900s. The trail follows the Cumberland Mountain ridge that marks the Kentucky/Virginia border.

Primitive campgrounds are located at Gibson Gap, about halfway between Pinnacle Overlook and the settlement, and at the settlement.

A park map will show you other trails to the settlement, from both the Kentucky and the Virginia sides of Cumberland Mountain.

The Ridge Trail is the longest of about 50 miles of hiking trails that traverse these wild mountains and provide the only access to some of the park's features, such as Sand Cave and White Rocks.

If you listen closely when the wind is right, you can still hear the murmur of Native American conversation, the shouts of mule drivers, the clink of trace chains, the distant boom of cannon.

Where: Extreme southwestern corner of state. Campground and picnic area on US 58 in Virginia; visitors center nearby on US 25E at Middlesboro, KY.

Hours: 8:00 A.M. until dusk year-round [visitors center open 9:00 A.M. to 5:00 P.M. daily November to April (except Christmas), 8:00 A.M. to 5 P.M. June to October]. Camping available year-round. Campfire programs, hikes, walks, music and craft demonstrations, other interpretive activities daily from mid-June to mid-August and weekends during spring and fall. Special programs for groups by prior arrangement with superintendent.

Admission: Free. Fee for summer shuttle, campsites, backcountry cabins.

Best time to visit: Anytime (especially when visibility is good) for scenic views. Mid-June to Labor Day and spring and fall weekends for interpretive programs.

Activities: Spectacular mountain vistas, visitors center and museum, self-guided nature trails and longer overnight trails, interpretive programs, campground, picnic areas, backcountry camping (permit required at visitors center), music and craft demonstrations, shuttle to settlement during summer.

Concessions: None.

Pets: Must be on leash.

Other: Motels in Middlesboro, KY, and Cumberland Gap, TN. Restaurants and grocery stores close to visitors center.

For more information:

Superintendent, Cumberland Gap National Historical Park, Box 1848, Middlesboro, KY 40965 (606-248-2817).

For organized tours (fee), contact Wilderness Road Tours (private enterprise), 224 Greenwood Road, Middlesboro, KY 40965 (606-248-2626).

DOUTHAT STATE PARK

Tucked into the faded folds of Bath and Alleghany Counties near the West Virginia line is fifty-acre Douthat Lake.

For more than half a century, Douthat State Park, which surrounds the lake, has attracted visitors the way a flower bed attracts bees. In summer, hundreds of thousands of people sample the trout fishing, the mountain camping, the good, solid food in the restaurant overlooking the lake, the sandy beach, and the rustic log and frame rental cabins built by the Civilian Conservation Corps in the 1930s.

Trout are stocked in the lake and its tributary, Wilson Creek, twice a week from the opening of trout season on the third Saturday in March through Labor Day.

The state park, a 4,493-acre National Historic Landmark and Virginia's oldest park, is also a hiker's delight, with its miles of foot trails that loop around and through the adjoining forest.

But Everette Mays, my companion on this trip, and I did not return to Douthat to hike, though in years past we've huffed and puffed up many of the steep trails and scrambled down several of the hemlock-shaded valleys.

This time, we were reliving memories of previous visits with respective family members. We had been coming here since 1970.

In years past, Everette and his father and my young son Anthony and I used to shoehorn ourselves into a johnboat and slowly troll Douthat Lake for trout. The electric motor hummed while Mepps spinners trailed behind the boat. In fact, the last good catch of rainbow trout I took from the lake had been with that foursome. Anthony would have been about ten. Today he's past thirty with a wife and five-year-old daughter.

Memories. Memories.

This chill and blustery April day, Everette and I were bundled up like Minnesota ice fishermen. We hooked the charged batteries to the electric motor, pointed the bow of the aluminum johnboat into the wind, and slowly trolled with spinners in the boat's wake.

We'd go for long periods without a strike, but that didn't seem to matter. A quiet lake surrounded by brooding mountains is a good place to simply be with a friend. But we finally caught trout (and I caught one chain pickerel) in this magnificent outdoor setting that we'd shared many times.

The sun dropped behind the western rim of the mountains. Patches of dark clouds — snow clouds, actually — stood out against the deepening blue sky. In the little stream below the dam, we quickly cleaned the five cold, firm rainbow trout we'd caught. Then our headlights illuminated the road out of the park, and we recalled all that Douthat had meant over the years.

Precious memories. They do linger.

Where: Bath County, five miles north of Clifton Forge. Take exit 27 off I-64 to County 629, then go four miles north.
Hours: Hiking trails 8:00 A.M. until dusk, year-round. Douthat Lake and Wilson Creek fishing closed February 1 until third Saturday in March. Campgrounds, cabins, boat rentals, restaurant seasonal. Swimming from Memorial Day to Labor Day.
Admission: Small parking fee. Swimming fee. Daily fishing fee from beginning of trout season in March to Labor Day; free after

Labor Day and free all year below dam. Fishing and trout licenses needed at all times to fish in lake and upper Wilson Creek. No trout license needed to fish below spillway. Licenses and permits available at camp store and boat dock.

Best time to visit: Third Saturday in March, when trout season opens, to Labor Day for fishing and camping. Anytime for scenery, wildlife, hiking. Spring through fall for other activities.

Activities: Hiking, self-guiding trails, tent and trailer campgrounds, picnicking, housekeeping cabins, swimming in rustic setting with sandy beach and bathhouse, paddleboat and rowboat rental (electric motors only) and boat ramp, lake and stream fishing (mainly for stocked trout), visitors center, interpretive programs, some handicapped facilities, environmental education center.

Concessions: Seasonal camp store, snack bar, restaurant.

Pets: On leash.

Other: Nearby Clifton Forge has laundromats, grocery stores, pharmacies.

For more information:

Douthat State Park, Route 1, Box 212, Millboro, VA 24460 (703-862-7200). For campground and cabin reservations, call 804-490-3939.

FAIRY STONE STATE PARK

The name of the park—Fairy Stone—invariably prompts questions.

Needless to say, there's a legend behind the name. Like most legends, the one involving Fairy Stone State Park ought to be approached with, shall we say, an open mind.

Suffice it to add that this legend, like most, takes in an enchanted forest with fairies, wood nymphs, naiads, and an elfin messenger who appeared to tell the others about the death of

Christ. When these magical beings cried, their tears fell upon the earth and crystallized to form little crosses.

The interesting part—the believable part—of the legend is that there really are little crystals in the shape of crosses. The crystals were formed when iron aluminum silicate experienced just the right combination of heat and pressure with the folding and crushing of the earth's crust during the creation of the Appalachian Mountains. You can find the crystals within the park. You can also buy them at local stores and wear them as jewelry. Even today, survivors of the Age of Aquarius believe that the crosses protect the wearer from evil, illness, or bad luck.

To find your own fairy stones, take State 346 out of the park and turn left on State 57. Go three miles to the first service station (Haynes 57) on the left. You may hunt the land on the left side of the service station.

Fairy Stone is one of Virginia's original six parks. It opened on June 15, 1936. At 4,868 acres, it was the largest then and is still one of the biggest parks. Now nearly sixty years old, the park is scheduled for renovation. There are plans to upgrade the cabins for year-round use, renovate the picnic area and beach buildings, and add underground electricity.

If you want to explore these gentle mountains, Fairy Stone has an interesting twenty-five miles of hiking and bicycle trails, ranging in difficulty from easy to strenuous.

The park lake was named a fishing hot spot by *Virginia Wildlife* magazine for its crappie, largemouth bass, bream, and channel catfish. The eleven-pound, four-ounce largemouth bass caught by one angler didn't hurt the lake's reputation either. Fishing traffic is medium on weekends and light during the week.

Two of our Richmond friends, Mike Flippen and Diane Montgomery, believe that heaven is a week's stay at Fairy Stone park in a lakeside cabin in spring when the rhododendrons are blooming, with a fire in the fireplace, two fishing rods, some live minnows for crappie, and minnows not-so-live for catfish.

Adjoining Fairy Stone Lake is big Philpott Reservoir, known by area fishermen for its lunker trout and largemouth bass, as well as a respectable smallmouth population. Fishing success varies from year to year. Several public recreation areas around Philpott Lake provide launch facilities for powerboats, and some have campgrounds and swimming beaches. The reservoir headquarters is located northwest of Bassett on County 904.

Fairy Stone Wildlife Management Area, managed by the Virginia Department of Game and Inland Fisheries, surrounds the park. Be on the lookout for deer, squirrels, doves, and ducks.

Where: Foothills of Blue Ridge Parkway in Patrick and Henry Counties, adjacent to Philpott Reservoir. From Stuart or Bassett, take State 57 to State 346 to the park.

Hours: Hiking, bicycle trails, boating 8:00 A.M. until dusk daily, year-round. Campgrounds open spring through fall. Visitors center, interpretive programs, swimming beach, concession area, weekends from Memorial Day to Labor Day.

Admission: Small parking fee. Fees for camping, cabin rental, swimming.

Best time to visit: Anytime for hiking, spring through fall for picnicking and camping, warm weather for fishing, summer for camping, interpretive programs, visitors center.

Activities: Hiking and bicycle trails, picnicking, swimming beach, boat launching (electric motors only on park lake), cabins, camping, fishing area with wheelchair access, amphitheater, visitors center, interpretive programs including guided fairy-stone hunts, nature hikes, bluegrass music.

Concessions: Concession area at swimming beach, rowboat and paddleboat rental.

Pets: Must be on leash.

Other: Bluegrass Festival in mid-May. Picturesque Mabry Mill and Virginia highlands village called Meadows of Dan are nearby. Martinsville and Stuart have grocery stores, post office. Fishing supplies and licenses in Bassett.

For more information:
Fairy Stone State Park, Route 2, Box 723, Stuart, VA 24171-9588 (703-930-2424 or 804-786-1712).

GEORGE WASHINGTON NATIONAL FOREST

Virginia is fortunate. Early in the 1900s, visionaries set aside huge portions of the state's northwestern mountain land surrounding the Shenandoah Valley.

The land eventually came to be called the George Washington National Forest. Today, with burgeoning development and skyrocketing land prices, the same purchase of public land would be all but impossible.

The George Washington National Forest is the crowning glory of Virginia's outdoor treasures. Beginning with the Blue Ridge mountain range, the George Washington National Forest spreads west over the West Virginia state line. It sprawls across more than a million acres of scenic mountains, pure rivers, and pastoral valleys. Fifty-seven million people live within a day's drive of some part of the million acres.

Take it from two who grew up in the Shenandoah Valley, surrounded by the George Washington. When you've never lived without vast public lands at your doorstep, it's all too easy to take for granted a certain freedom the national forest affords.

In much of the western portion of the state, where the combined George Washington and Jefferson National Forests total about 1.7 million acres, walking out the back door and prowling endless woods is second nature, no landowner permission required. That changed when we moved near Richmond. We quickly learned that there are no vast portions of public, or open, land east of the Blue Ridge range. And private land in eastern Virginia, like private land everywhere, is posted tighter than a loan shark's smile.

So we make pilgrimages, so to speak, to the George Washington as often as we can. We return to these woods to wade icy streams for trout. To camp beneath hemlocks. To hear the sharp warning bark of a chipmunk and the "perks" of a hen turkey. To hike the countless trails that lace the forest like spiderwebs, knowing some of them to be the same buffalo paths and Native American trails walked by George Washington, Stonewall Jackson, and Robert E. Lee.

We come back to flush ruffed grouse or maybe woodcock and then cool tired feet in the clear water of a mountain lake. We sit on high peaks and gaze off into valleys, or drive hundreds of miles of back roads along rivers and ridge lines, where we sometimes encounter no one else for half a day.

We come in spring, and our senses are revived with the tangy flavor of wild strawberries and blueberries, the sight of blossoming dogwood, shadbush and redbud, and the sound at dawn of a many-voiced bird chorus in the treetop canopy — robins, blackbirds, cardinals, phoebes, bluebirds.

By fall, it's a different world, when entire fields turn yellow with tickseed sunflower and country roadsides are spattered with purple aster, wild red raspberries, drooping goldenrod, and Queen Anne's lace. The gorgeous foliage of mid-October reflected in deep-green forest rivers and lakes turns up in many photo album pictures.

Sure, we'll share it with you. There's more than enough to go around.

What's Available

You are allowed to camp anywhere in the national forest, unless an area is specifically posted otherwise. Campers are urged to practice "no-trace ethics": protect streams and living vegetation, bury human waste at least eight inches deep, and pack out

A black bear cub in a quandry

THREE BEARS OR MORE

Black bears will not stand around for a nose count, so doing a census on them is like guessing the number of marbles in a glass jar. A lot of what you're trying to count is hidden.

Nevertheless, the return of the black bear to significant numbers in Virginia is one of several quiet wildlife-management success stories.

With a sanctuary (Shenandoah National Park) and at least two major mountain ranges to wander (the Blue Ridge and the Allegheny), black bear have been protected and studied in great depth by biologists. In areas with a surplus of bear, several hundred have been harmlessly live-trapped and resettled in mountain sections, principally the southwestern part of the state, where the big animals had all but disappeared.

Perhaps, in the East, bears are associated with Smoky Mountain National Park in North Carolina and Tennessee. But, with the capture and relocation program in Virginia, coupled with stringent hunting seasons where bears were scarce, the state now has a healthy bear population. If you're in the right place at the right time, there's a chance you'll see a bear shuffling along.

Don't bet on winter, when bears are often asleep for days, even weeks. Instead, try waiting beside a mountaintop blueberry patch in spring. And in autumn, bears get a strong case of the prowls and sometimes even wander into city limits.

The very best place in the state to see bears is Shenandoah National Park, where they aren't hunted. Biologists say the population in the park is higher per square mile than in any other place in Virginia. The Great Dismal Swamp is also a good place to see them. So are the back roads that thread the mountains of Highland, Bath, and Rockingham Counties.

For the most part, though, bears are reclusive animals. Their presence is given away by their habit of walking in their own tracks until, over time, depressions are worn along a trail in the shape of their huge footprints. Also look for their claw marks on tree trunks, and for rotted stumps and logs they've torn apart for a meal of ants.

whatever you pack in. In addition, there are twenty-seven developed campgrounds, where there may be a small fee. Most have water and toilet facilities, along with tables, fire rings or grills, and tent pads or trailer spaces.

You can spend a lifetime exploring the 950 miles of hiking trails here, including 61.9 miles of the white-blazed Appalachian Trail. Most of the recreation areas have bulletin boards near their entrances to show the trails, and maps may be requested from the district offices.

Canoeing, rafting, float fishing, and tubing are attractions on several rivers, especially the South Fork of the Shenandoah.

Bring your mountain bicycle to old, abandoned forest roads for a great way to get into the backwoods. Rangers at district offices can recommend the best paths.

Trail Specialist Al McPherson suggests a way to stay fit and perform a service at the same time: adopt a section of trail. "In this time of shrinking government [subsidies], we are relying more and more on the folks we serve to help us maintain what we have. Our employees could not keep up maintenance without the help of individual volunteers and groups like the various Appalachian Trail clubs."

For newcomers, the thing to remember is this: when in doubt, contact the forest service supervisor's office. Ask for the color brochure on the George Washington. It includes a map, plus all the general information to get you started. Then, when you choose a specific area of this outdoor lover's paradise to visit, you may want to contact a local ranger district office. Addresses and phone numbers are:

Campground reservations (800-280-2267) or, for hearing and speech impaired (800-879-4496).

Supervisor, George Washington National Forest, Harrison Plaza, Harrisonburg, VA 22801 (703-564-8300).

Deerfield Ranger District, U.S. Forest Service, Route 6, Box 419, Staunton, VA 24401 (703-885-8028).

Dry River Ranger District, U.S. Forest Service, 112 North River Road, Bridgewater, VA 22812 (703-828-2591).

James River Ranger District, U.S. Forest Service, 810-A Madison Avenue, Covington, VA 24426 (703-962-2214).

Lee Ranger District, U.S. Forest Service, Windsor Knit Road, Route 4, Box 515, Edinburg, VA 22824 (703-984-4101).

Pedlar Ranger District, U.S. Forest Service, 2424 Magnolia Avenue, Buena Vista, VA 24416 (703-261-6105).

Warm Springs Ranger District, U.S. Forest Service, Highway 220 South, Route 2, Box 30, Hot Springs, VA 24445 (703-839-2521).

Points of Interest

Appalachian Trail — Some sixty miles of this famous Georgia-to-Maine trail follow the Blue Ridge range through the George Washington National Forest. See heading in chapter 1.

Chessie Nature Trail — Between Lexington and Buena Vista, just west of the George Washington's Pedlar Ranger District, is this seven-mile path following an old railroad grade along the Maury River. Beginning at the Virginia Military Institute Island, you pass by several old canal locks and other historic sites. Wildflowers and birds of the woodlands, cliffs, and open fields are a spring bonus. As many as fifty-three different bird species have been recorded in May alone. Lexington Visitor Center (703-463-3777).

Crabtree Falls — Located east of the Blue Ridge Parkway off State 56 and just one-half mile north of the Appalachian Trail in Nelson County are five major waterfalls and several smaller ones that drop a total of 1,200 feet. You can park at the bottom, off the winding little mountain road (State 56), take the arched wooden bridge spanning the Tye River, and walk 700 feet to the first of several overlooks to view the falls, and then choose whether or not to continue the more strenuous climb to the top.

Or you can come in on County 826, a rugged dirt road that leads to the top of Crabtree Meadows. The falls are generally prettiest in spring when the water is high. Obey all warning signs. Twenty-one hikers have been swept over the falls to their deaths by venturing too close. Pedlar Ranger District (703-261-6105).

Goshen Pass — Take State 39 north of Lexington, between sections of the George Washington National Forest, to see what happens when the Maury River is forced between two mountains at Goshen Pass. Many tubers, waders, anglers, and picnickers enjoy the big boulders and rapids here.

Henry Lanum Jr. Trail (formerly Pompey and Mount Pleasant Trail) — This Appalachian Trail spur in Amherst County, nine miles east of Buena Vista, is a five-mile loop gradually ascending Pompey Mountain (4,032 feet), then continuing along the ridgetop to a companion peak, Mount Pleasant. The path follows old forest roads through patches of wildflowers, blueberries, mountain laurel, and rhododendron and stands of chestnut oak, scarlet oak, pignut hickory, and yellow birch. Panoramic vistas. From Buena Vista, take US 60 east across Blue Ridge Parkway to County 634. Follow 634 north to Forest Road 48. Go right on 48 and left on Forest Road 51. Trailhead parking area is on 51. Pedlar Ranger District (703-261-6105).

Hidden Valley — This campground in remote Bath County, six miles northwest of Hot Springs and north of State 39, includes pastures and farmland in a secluded valley with an excellent trout stream and hiking trails. Nearby is historic antebellum Warwick Mansion, site of the motion picture *Sommersby,* starring Jodie Foster and Richard Gere. The mansion has been restored as the

Hidden Valley Bed and Breakfast (703-839-3178). A couple of buildings from the movie set remain. Warm Springs Ranger District (703-839-2521).

Highland Scenic Tour — This twenty-mile scenic loop in Alleghany and Rockbridge Counties is one of more than 100 designated National Forest Scenic Byways in the country. Located

A wood nymph butterfly on butterfly weed

off I-64 between exits 35 and 43 and between Lexington and Covington, it includes about nine miles of paved County 850, four miles of graveled County 770, and seven miles of graveled Forest Road 447. Many table mountain and pitch pine trees on the ridges are up to 150 years old.

Enjoy the rugged mountain landscape, but do not expect amenities or signs; the tour is just now being developed. County 770 and Forest Road 447 may be impassable in winter. Towed vehicles are not recommended on the steep hairpin turns of County 770.

Foot trails off County 850 lead into the 6,450-acre Rich Hole Wilderness. Nearby (one mile west of I-64, exit 35, and eight miles east of Covington on US 60) is the Longdale Recreation Area, with a picnic shelter, small swimming lake with sandy beach, and hiking trails. James River Ranger District (703-962-2214).

Lake Moomaw — This 2,500-acre mountain lake in Alleghany and Bath Counties has swimming, boating, fishing, waterskiing, sailing, and camping. See heading in Chapter 1.

Laurel Fork — Coming to this elevated northwest Highland County ridge on the West Virginia line is a bit like a visit to Canada. Those outsized rabbit tracks in the snow were left by the big hind feet of the aptly named snowshoe hare. Also called the varying hare for its color change from white in winter to brown in summer, the showshoe is found nowhere else in Virginia. Beaver are prevalent in the western part of the area.

Snow and ice linger here far longer than in the valleys, and red spruce and hardwood trees (birch, cherry, maple, and beech) typical of northern forests cover the ridge. Thirty species of plants and animals considered rare in Virgina inhabit Laurel Fork, including (in addition to the snowshoe) the northern flying squirrel and the fisher.

From Staunton, take US 250 into West Virginia to its

intersection with State 28. Go north (right) on 28 about six miles to Forest Road 106 and the signs for Locust Springs Recreation Area. Follow signs for parking and access to northern section of the area.

To access the southern portion, take US 250 to Hightown. Go north (right) on State 640 to Blue Grass, then west (left) on State 642. Proceed about nine miles to intersection with Forest Road 457, turn right on 457 for parking. Warm Springs Ranger District (703-839-2521).

Massanutten Mountain and Fort Valley — This unusual canoe-shaped valley surrounded by mountains is set within the much larger Shenandoah Valley and bordered by the north and south forks of the legendary Shenandoah River. Fort Valley was named by George Washington, who planned to use it as a winter retreat if he were defeated by the British at Yorktown.

To reach this remote and gentle valley from I-81, take the New Market exit east on US 211 to New Market Gap, and look for the visitors center on the right. Close by are several trails, two of them paved and suitable for wheelchairs.

An interpretive trail for the blind, built in cooperation with the Lions Club, is about eight miles northeast of US 211 on Forest Road 274. Camping is permitted in summer at Elizabeth Furnace at the north end of the valley.

For more information; contact the Massanutten Visitor Center (open April to November), Route 1, Box 100, New Market, VA 22844 (703-740-8310) or Lee Ranger District (703-984-4101).

North Mountain Trail — This fourteen-mile backcountry trail winds along the crest of Great North Mountain west of Buffalo Gap in Augusta County. The trail passes just below Elliott Knob—at 4,463 feet, it is the highest point in the George Washington National Forest.

Spectacular views in all directions, including the lovely

Deerfield Valley, are the reward for negotiating the often steep and rugged terrain. Deerfield Ranger District (703-885-8028).

Ramsey's Draft Wilderness Area — Seven trails lead into this 6,519-acre mountainous wilderness, where you can hike along clear streams with pools of native trout to huge virgin hemlock stands. You'll splash through the shallow stream several times, so wear wading shoes.

Ask a ranger for directions to the black birch with a fourteen-foot circumference, selected for the Virginia Register of Big Trees. Deerfield Ranger District (703-885-8028).

Reddish Knob — From high atop Shenandoah Mountain (elevation 4,397 feet) in the northern tip of Augusta County on the West Virginia line, you can view the South Branch Valley to the west and the Shenandoah Valley to the east.

Hang gliders launch from this knob. The rare Cow Knob salamander can be found along this ridge. Dry River District (703-828-2214).

Saint Mary's Wilderness Area — This mountainous gorge formed by the clear tumbling waters of St. Mary's River in Augusta County funnels visitors onto one main trail, which is rapidly becoming overused. This path leads upstream from a lower parking lot to a double waterfall. The climb past the falls up to Green Pond in Big Levels is steep and rugged. A side trail below the falls up Mine Bank Creek leads to the Blue Ridge Parkway. Allow about three hours for the round trip to the falls. Forest service personnel ask that hikers help protect this fragile place.

Although the area is designated wilderness, other parts of the national forest may provide a more remote experience.

Ask a ranger for directions from the Raphine exit of I-81 to St. Mary's lower parking area on Forest Road 41, northeast of the little town of Vesuvius. Pedlar Ranger District (703-261-6105).

Sherando Lake – This recreation area, built by the Civilian Conservation Corps, is fourteen miles south of Waynesboro off County 664, within the 30,000-acre Big Levels Wildlife Management Area. Gates are open from 6:00 A.M. to 10:00 P.M. daily, year-round.

An upper and lower lake (seven and twenty-four acres, respectively) in hollows of the Blue Ridge provide freshwater fishing, boating, and swimming. Campgrounds are open from April 1 to October 31. A campground for hunters is available during hunting season. There are lakeside and mountain hiking trails, picnicking, summer amphitheater evening programs, and a visitors center. Although there is no launch ramp, small boats without motors may be carried to the water. User fee. Pedlar Ranger District (703-261-6105).

Todd Lake – This recreation area is in northwestern Augusta County, west of Stokesville and north of West Augusta, on the Skidmore Fork of the North River. From US 250, just east of West Augusta, go north on County 715 which becomes Forest Road 96. Go right on Forest Road 95 to Todd Lake. Activities include camping, hiking, and lake swimming; showers are available. User fee. The twenty-seven-mile Wild Oak National Recreation Trail starts near here.

Also nearby, on Forest Road 96, near the junction with Forest Road 95, is fifty-one-acre Elkhorn Lake, well known to trout fishermen (no gasoline-powered boats). Dry River Ranger District (703-828-2214). East of Todd Lake, outside the national forest near Mount Solon, is Natural Chimneys, where seven limestone towers rise 120 feet above the surrounding land. Call 703-350-2510 for information.

GRAYSON HIGHLANDS STATE PARK

Pull your chair a little closer to the hearth. Here, have a little more coffee. We have a special treat in mind. We're going to tell you about Grayson Highlands—one of our favorite places in all Virginia.

Consider this a gift from the heart. Our hope is that as you read this, it is late spring in the southern highlands, when the thin, high call of the golden-crowned kinglet marks an invisible but unmistakable boundary to others of its kind. Spring is especially memorable in the mountain hollows. The understory of dark green rhododendron droops heavily with blossoms of fragrant pink over pristine, clear mountain streams, where native brook trout dart beneath rocks to avoid the kingfisher's dive.

Or maybe you'll arrive in summer, when oppressive heat and humidity make you long for the relief of nature's sweet, cool washcloth on your forehead. In this place high in the alpine meadows, the average temperature is never above seventy-two degrees, and a blanket at night feels good.

On the other hand, autumn would be fine. For it is then that the red maple and yellow birch splash their namesake colors across dark spruces that march off down the mountainsides, outlining elegant spires against faraway mountains and azure blue skies.

Perhaps, though, we should wish for you that it is winter, when the air crackles with cold and the grassy balds are left mostly to the sleeping bear, the silent snow, the whisper of a raven's wing.

The Highlands

The name "highlands" is apt. The altitude is 3,700 feet at the entrance to this 4,754-acre park, where hillside meadows slant upward toward evergreen forests. As you drive up the winding road to the visitors center on Haw Orchard Mountain, the craggy rock outcropping of Twin Pinnacles comes into view. Take the short trail to the summit of Little Pinnacle, and you'll be standing close to a mile above sea level and about 1,400 feet above the park entrance. In the distance to the northwest is Mount Rogers, the highest point in Virginia at 5,729 feet, and 640 feet higher than where you're standing.

Despite the height of Mount Rogers, it's covered with trees and there's no view. Just turn around and take a short hike southeast to Big Pinnacle. On a clear day, the 360-degree view will take your breath away. You'll be glad you packed your camera and/or binoculars. Far below you'll hear Cabin Creek rushing down to the valley.

If you want to stand atop Mount Rogers proper, and if you have an extra five to six hours, you can walk there and back from the park. The affable Grayson Highlands park manager, Harvey Thompson, will be glad to describe the hike from Grayson, which he says is the "least strenuous access to Mount Rogers from any direction." Get a map along with the illustrated, informative booklet about Grayson trails from the office or visitors center.

Mount Rogers Hike

Several trails start from the Massie Gap parking area, including the Rhododendron Trail. Follow this trail through the meadow to the north, across a rail fence, and over the hill to Sullivan Swamp. Along the way, you may see ponies that remind you of the wild ponies of Chincoteague Island on the Eastern Shore. At Grayson Highlands, the ponies have been turned loose to keep the high country open by grazing these remote grassy ridges year-round.

Then it's a rugged two-and-a-half-mile trek over the rocks and open slopes of windswept Wilburn Ridge to connect with the famous Appalachian Trail, or you can take an earlier connection around the left side of Wilburn Ridge. A left turn on the

Appalachian Trail leads to the Lewis Fork Wilderness and to the Mount Rogers Trail, where the path leads you up and into a spruce-fir forest, rare so far south of Canada.

Be sure to follow all guidelines for wilderness hiking, including carrying water, a whistle, and an extra jacket. A topographic map is not a bad idea, either. Sudden temperature drops and weather changes are common. In a matter of minutes, fog can sweep in to obscure all familiar landmarks.

As you hike the Grayson trails, go softly and stop to listen. A curious white-tailed deer may sneak up behind you as you eat your lunch under a big white oak. Wild turkeys may be heard scratching in the leaves in a thicket of mountain laurel. In spring and early summer, a ruffed grouse may break the stillness with the explosive sound of drumming on an old chestnut log. A black bear or bobcat may even cross your path.

If you are on horseback, a campground and stable will give you and your horse a place to stay after riding the trails. You'll have two miles of scenic Grayson horse trails to explore, and access to the Virginia Highlands Horse Trail in the Jefferson National Forest.

Where: Grayson County, less than three miles from North Carolina border. From I-81 at Marion, take State 16 south to Volney and US 58 west to the park.

Hours: 8:00 A.M. until dusk daily, year-round. Campgrounds open spring through fall; check park for exact dates.

Admission: Small parking fee.

Best time to visit: Late spring for rhododendron and wildflower bloom, summer for alpine air-conditioning, fall for foliage.

Activities: Hiking, including access to Appalachian Trail and self-guided trail, bridle trail, camping (electric and water hookups planned for forty sites), alpine scenery, wildlife observation, visitors center, amphitheater programs, trout fishing, closely regulated hunting area, picnic area next to rebuilt homestead site with two log cabins, springhouse, cane mill.

Concessions: Camp store, craft shop, stables to board horses.
Pets: Must be on leash.
Other: Mount Rogers National Recreation Area northwest of park; Little Creek Wilderness northeast of park
For more information:

Grayson Highlands State Park, Route 2, Box 141, Mouth of Wilson, VA 24363 (703-579-7092).

HUNGRY MOTHER STATE PARK

In our memories, Hungry Mother Lake was a summer place of blue-green tranquillity with a gently sinuous shoreline tracing the soft folds of Brushy Mountain.

We'd been there before, several times, but always when children ran diving into the water from the sandy beach, when rowboats and paddleboats dotted the surface of the lake, and parking lots were overflowing.

So it was serendipitous to come upon the lake in winter. We came down Walker Mountain from the north, where a sudden half-inch covering of hoarfrost made the fog-shrouded mountaintop a fairyland. As the 108-acre lake came into view, ice gleamed in stark contrast to the dark, naked trees rising up the mountains around the edge. Skaters glided across the lake's smooth surface. Obviously, our memories had been incomplete.

Virginia winters are not always mindful of those who love skating on ice, but when it gets cold enough, Hungry Mother Lake is like a Currier and Ives painting.

As legend has it, the creek that was later dammed to form the lake was named Hungry Mother after a small child was found wandering through the colonial wilderness, uttering only the words "hungry . . . mother." A search party later discovered the child's mother, dead at the foot of a mountain. She'd collapsed from hunger after she and her daughter escaped from Native Americans who had kidnapped them.

The focus of the 2,200-acre state park is water activities and appreciation of the woodlands around the park. The last two state-record northern pike were caught here. The most recent was a forty-eight-inch fish weighing twenty-seven pounds, twelve ounces.

Although seven Virginia state parks have bridle trails, Hungry Mother is the only park with rental horses. There are twelve miles of scenic bridle and hiking trails.

Housekeeping cabins with fireplaces are available for rent on a weekly basis from spring through fall; included are rustic log cabins built by the Civilian Conservation Corps during the Great Depression.

Hemlock Haven, the Virginia state park system's first conference center, provides a beautiful setting for day or overnight conferences, banquets, family reunions, and company picnics. Facilities include small and large meeting rooms, full-service catering, modern lighted tennis courts, a sports complex, a swimming pool, heated housekeeping cabins, and conference lodges.

Where: Southwestern Virginia, north of Marion in Smyth County. From I-81, take exit 47 and go south on US 11 toward Marion. Turn right on State 16 and go four miles to the park.

Hours: 8:00 A.M. until dark daily, year-round. Campgrounds and housekeeping cabins late May to September (dates may vary from year to year). Horseback riding, swimming, interpretive programs, visitors center, Memorial Day to Labor Day weekend.

Admission: Small parking fee. Fees for horseback riding, cabin rental, swimming, boat launching, camping (hookups extra).

Best time to visit: Early to mid-May for rhododendron bloom and wildflowers, mid-July for weekend arts and crafts festival, fall for foliage, some winters for ice skating and cross-country skiing.

Activities: Excellent freshwater fishing, wheelchair-accessible fishing pier, horseback riding, camping, hiking, picnicking, swimming beach and bathhouse, boat launch (no gasoline motors), interpretive programs, visitors center, cross-country skiing, ice skating, canoe and paddleboat tours.

Concessions: Seasonal rowboat, paddleboat, and canoe rental, horse rental, camp store, snack bar. Restaurant open Mother's Day through Labor Day.

Pets: Must be on leash.

Other: Hungry Mother Arts and Crafts Festival, third weekend in July. Marion has grocery stores, motels, restaurants. Oby's on US 11 north has a friendly staff and low-priced buffet featuring home cooking.

For more information:

Hungry Mother State Park, Route 5, Box 109, Marion, VA 24354 (703-783-3422 or 804-786-1712).

JEFFERSON NATIONAL FOREST

From the James River, which more or less splits Virginia east to west, to the southwestern tip of the state some 218 miles away, a treasure trove of forests, lakes, campgrounds, trout streams, wilderness areas, mountain balds, and scenery takes your breath away.

Best of all, this is public land. That means you don't need the landowner's permission to explore the lovely grandeur that's home to black bear, ruffed grouse, white-tailed deer, beaver, and wild turkey.

We refer, of course, to the Jefferson National Forest, with its 710,000 acres of wonderfully diverse animal and plant communities. The variations in elevation across the Jefferson assure that you'll crisscross several different worlds if you cover it all.

Plants and animals found along the banks of the James

River at 600 feet above sea level are different in many cases from what you'll encounter at the windswept crest of 5,729-foot Mount Rogers, the highest point in Virginia. Both are in Jefferson National Forest.

Consider the vast forest cover. It's mostly Appalachian mixed hardwood (beech, oak, and hickory, for example) mingled with conifers (evergreen cone bearers such as pine and spruce). But there's so much flowering vegetation that, except in the dead of winter, something always is either blooming or showing spring and fall color. And on the highest peaks, there are isolated stands of Canadian red spruce left from the last ice age 10,000 years ago.

Wildlife is as varied and abundant as anywhere in the Middle Atlantic states. Big-game hunting for deer, bear, and turkey is serious business in the forest during the two months of the Virginia hunting season (roughly November and December). Grouse, squirrel, and dove are also hunted in season.

But wildlife watching, as opposed to hunting, is also popular throughout the Jefferson National Forest. More than 160 species of birds live here or migrate through the forest. Listen for the plaintive high calls of the white-throated sparrow in winter and the wood pewee in summer. Another winter visitor is the brown creeper, an inconspicuous little bird that creeps up a tree trunk looking for insects, then flies to the base of another tree and starts up again. A small, acrobatic bird heading down the tree is most likely the white-breasted nuthatch, with its nasal "yank-yank" call.

If you like to doze off to the haunting sound of whippoor-wills in the evening, the forest is a camper's delight. You can pitch a tent beside any of the hundreds of roads and trails inside the forest, so long as you don't block anyone else, or the area isn't specifically marked "no camping." District rangers will be happy to recommend some of the most desirable spots away from established campgrounds. The night sky in the mountains, away from

A gray squirrel

ANIMAL SIGN

When nothing is moving in the woods except an occasional bird, it's easy to assume there's no ineresting wildlife to obseve. So go somewhere else, right?

Maybe not. First, look a little closer. Walk a little slower. There—in the mud. A critter with a webbed foot and five toes has left a print by the riverbank. Nearby is another tiny footprint. A few yards upriver, a small pile of debris has been scraped together beside the trail. On both sides of the river are chutes where something's been sliding into the water on a regular basis.

The walking trail leaves the riverbank and angles up a steep bank. Near the top is a mangled beech sapling, its bark hanging in shreds. And what's this bare spot on the forest floor where the leaves have been scraped back? In fact, a thirty-yard swath on this ridge is ragged with what must have been vigorous scratchings.

Then, farther along, under a big, craggy white oak, is a tightly packed, four-inch-long clump of gray hair and tiny bones.

Tracks . . . water slide . . . debris pile . . . the mangled tree . . . the hairball—all clues to a mystery. As it turns out, along this particular section of trail are the track, water slide, and scent mound of beaver. The tiny footprints were made by a pine vole. A whitetail buck rubbed his antlers against the sapling. The torn-up leaf cover on the forest floor was made by a flock of foraging wild turkeys. The hair and bone clump was the undigested remains of a meal of a great horned owl roosting on a branch overhead.

The trail is nothing out of the ordinary. In fact, it's the one behind our home near the South Anna River in central Virginia. We walk the trail daily. But only on days when we are not rushed do we see such a bonanza of wildlife sign.

Since most wild things depend on secrecy for survival, actual sightings of bear, bobcat, fox, owl, raccoon, and many other animals are unusual in many areas. Deer are less spooky.

We've found that the more we learn about the tracks, droppings, depressions, scrapes, burrows, gnawings, and nests that these animals leave behind, the more we enjoy our trips to the woods. The more we see, the more there is to see. Even the way a blade of grass is chewed, cut, or torn can reveal secrets.

We use every available source to help us unravel the clues,

checking bookstores and libraries. Here are three of our favorite sources:

"Animal Tracks—And How to Know Them" by J. J. Shomon, a free printout available from the Virginia Department of Game and Inland Fisheries, Information Department, 4010 West Broad Street, P.O. Box 11104, Richmond, VA 23230-1104 (804-367-1000).

A Field Guide to Animal Tracks by Olaus J. Murie, Peterson Field Guide Series, published by Houghton Mifflin Company.

Tom Brown's Field Guide to Nature Observation and Tracking by Tom Brown Jr., published by Berkley Books.

---

city lights, is a dome of thousands of stars, brilliant all the way to the horizon.

Spread throughout the Jefferson Forest are sixteen developed campgrounds with 580 campsites. Campgrounds have tent pads, cooking grills, picnic tables, and toilets; some have hot-water showers, fishing lakes, beaches, amphitheaters, and naturalist programs. One group picnic area can handle 400 people.

Trailers up to twenty-two feet can be accommodated at certain areas. Central dumping stations are provided, but no water or electric hookups are available.

Developed campsites throughout the national forest are available on a first-come, first-served basis. Reservations are not required. Horses aren't allowed in campgrounds; however, several ranger districts provide special camping areas for those who bring horses to get around on in the forest.

You may see areas of defoliation in the Jefferson caused by a variety of pests, including the gypsy moth, the southern pine beetle, and the hemlock wooly adelgid. Researchers are scrambling to find ways to curb the spread of these insects without harming other plants and animals.

For a color brochure featuring a map and general information, first contact the supervisor's office. Then you may want to use the brochure to contact individual ranger districts in the area you wish to visit.

Contact the forest service weekdays from 8:00 A.M. to 4:30 P.M. at these addresses:

Forest Supervisor, Jefferson National Forest, 5162 Valley-pointe Parkway, Roanoke, VA 24019 (703-265-6054).

Blacksburg Ranger District, U.S. Forest Service, 110 South-park Drive, Blacksburg, VA 24060 (703-552-4641). (To reach the office three miles northwest of Blacksburg, use US 460.)

Clinch Ranger District, 9416 Darden Drive, Wise, VA 24293 (703-328-2931). (The office is on County 646, across from Clinch Valley College.)

Glenwood Ranger District, Highway 130, P.O. Box 10, Natural Bridge Station, VA 24579 (703-291-2189). (The office is on County 130, 1.5 miles east of Natural Bridge.)

New Castle Ranger District, Box 246, New Castle, VA 24127 (703-864-5195). (The office is two miles east of New Castle on County 615.)

Wythe Ranger District, 155 Sherwood Forest Road, Wythe-ville, VA 24382 (703-228-5551). (The office is on US 11 west of Wytheville.)

Points of Interest

Appalachian Trail — Passing along ridgetops of the Jefferson are 280 miles of the white-blazed Appalachian Trail, which extends from Maine to Georgia. See heading in Chapter 1.

Barbours Creek Wilderness — This mountainous terrain covers 5,700 acres of northernmost Craig County at the border of Alleghany and Botetourt Counties. Nearby on County 617 is the Lipes Branch Hiking and Horse Trail and The Pines camp-ground, complete with horse corral and unloading ramp.

A few miles to the east, on County 685 north of Barbours Creek, is the Fenwick Mines Wetlands, with family camping, a ballfield, picnic tables, and hiking trails. The Fenwick Forest Walk is an easy, one-mile interpretive hike along Mill Creek; the Fenwick Wetlands Trail is a half-mile, wheelchair-accessible path winding through open forest and wetlands. A side trail leads to a wetlands observation deck. New Castle Ranger District (703-864-5195).

Bark Camp Lake — A forty-five-acre lake southeast of Tacoma in northern Scott County, this is a good warm- and cold-water fishery for northern pike, bass, sunfish, and catfish, and it has put-and-take trout fishing. Camping, hiking, picnicking, and boating (electric motors only) are available. Clinch Ranger District (703-328-2931).

Beartown Wilderness Area — Some of the most remote and steep woods of the Jefferson are in these 5,609 acres on the southeastern border of Tazewell County, west of Burkes Garden. There are no improved roads to the wilderness. The few primitive roads remaining are being reclaimed by natural vegetation. You can get into the southern edge of Beartown from the Appalachian Trail where it traverses Chestnut Ridge on Garden Mountain.

The changing elevation up to 4,400 feet allows diverse growth, including Appalachian hardwoods similar to the woods of Georgia, as well as hemlocks and northern hardwoods. On the ridge is a quaking bog and spruce-fir forest more typical of Canada. When the bog is dry, you can feel it quaver as you walk on it. Ask a ranger for directions to the extensive beaver ponds and bog, and to Roaring Fork Creek, which has native trout. Wythe Ranger District (703-228-5551).

Cascades National Recreation Trail — This moderately strenuous hike up Little Stony Creek will bring you to a sixty-six-foot waterfall. Allow about three hours for the round-trip. The trail begins at the Cascades picnic area. Take US 460 west from Blacksburg to Pembroke. Turn right on County 623 and go three and a half miles; follow the signs. Blacksburg Ranger District (703-552-4641).

Clinch Mountain Wildlife Management Area — This 25,000-acre mountainous area (elevations of 2,200 to 4,600 feet) north of Saltville touches four counties: Smyth, Washington, Russell, and Tazewell.

Diverse habitats include desert-like cliffs, grasslands, rivers, streams, a lake, and beaver ponds. At various altitudes are southern Appalachian hardwoods, northern bogs, northern hardwoods, and spruce. For a small fee between late March and Labor Day, you can fish for stocked trout in mountaintop 330-acre Laurel Bed Lake (launching ramp) and for native trout above the lake in Big Tumbling Creek. Big Tumbling Creek Falls is located on County 747 leading up Clinch Mountain toward the lake and primitive campground.

In addition to excellent fishing opportunities, popular activities include horseback riding, canoeing, bird-watching, berry picking, herbing (permit required), and wildlife observation (beaver, rabbit, mink, raccoon, fox, squirrel, quail, ruffed grouse, wild turkey, deer, and black bear). The campground is open during fishing season; there is a small fee.

Contact Hungry Mother State Park, Route 5, Box 109, Marion, VA 24354 (703-783-3422). Also, Virginia Department of Game and Inland Fisheries, P.O. Box 11104, Richmond, VA 23230-1104 (804-367-1000).

High Knob — From this 4,160-foot peak with an observation tower on Stone Mountain in Wise County, five states can be seen—Virginia, West Virginia, Kentucky, Tennessee, and North

Carolina. High Knob Recreation Area has a four-acre lake with swimming beach, picnicking, camping, fishing, amphitheater programs, hot showers, lakeside hiking, a hiking trail to the tower, and a nineteen-mile hike southeast through Edith Gap to Bark Camp Lake and Recreation Area in Scott County. Clinch Ranger District (703-328-2931).

Highlands Gateway Visitor Center — This facility provides information on the Jefferson National Forest and surrounding areas. From I-81 in Wythe County take the Fort Chiswell exit (exit 80) onto State 121; follow information area signs to Fort Chiswell Factory Merchants Mall and the visitors center (703-637-6766).

James River Face and Thunder Ridge Wilderness Areas — South of the James River in Bedford, Rockbridge, and Botetourt Counties, these two areas encompass 11,500 acres of rugged high-mountain terrain as primitive and untouched as any in this part of the state. Several maintained trails lead in all directions from the center of James River Face wilderness, and the white-blazed Appalachian Trail intersects it.

The James River turns violent as it funnels over Balcony Falls at Glasgow through a gorge between James River Face and Three Sisters Knobs to the north. From State 130 at Natural Bridge Station, County 759 leads to the trailheads.

Established campgrounds and picnic area are available at nearby Cave Mountain Lake. Forest Road 35 leads between the two wilderness areas from the Blue Ridge Parkway and Appalachian Trail. Also, if you follow the Appalachian Trail or the parkway south from Thunder Ridge, you can access the rugged trail to Apple Orchard Falls. Start from the Sunset Field overlook on the parkway near milepost 78. It's a little more than a mile to a steep descent from which you can look back at the 200-foot falls. Glenwood Ranger District (703-291-2188).

Lake Keokee — This ninety-two-acre lake is eleven miles south-west of Appalachia (pronounced Ap-a-LAT-chee by residents) in Lee County. You may have all to yourself the easy four-mile loop trail circling the lake, passing mostly through hardwood forest. Activities include hiking, picnicking, wildlife observation, boat launching, and fishing for muskie, largemouth bass, catfish and sunfish.

On the south side of the lake near the dam, a spur from the lake trail leads south through Olinger Gap to connect with the fourteen-mile Stone Mountain Trail, on which you will pass a stand of old-growth hemlock (more than 300 years old), many miniature waterfalls, and high rock outcroppings with scenic vistas. At the west end of the Stone Mountain Trail is Cave Springs Recreation Area on County 621, with shaded campsites and a small lake for swimming. Clinch Ranger District (703-328-2931).

Little Stony National Recreation Trail — You can take this easy three-mile trail with short, rough, rocky sections to Hanging Rock picnic area in northern Scott County south of Coeburn. There is abundant hemlock, mountain laurel, and rhododendron along a deep canyon, and two cascading waterfalls on Little Stony Creek. Clinch Ranger District (703-328-2931).

Mountain Lake Wilderness Area — This 11,113-acre wilderness, the largest in the Jefferson National Forest, takes its name from nearby Mountain Lake, the only natural lake in western Virginia. Hikers may follow the War Spur and Chestnut Trail and access the Appalachian Trail from the wilderness.

As you ascend the road to the War Spur parking lot, you'll pass Mountain Lake Resort. If it looks familiar, you saw it in the movie *Dirty Dancing*, which was filmed here. The lake was created by a long-ago landslide and is situated on a highland plateau on the eastern Continental Divide. Waters east of this plateau flow to the Atlantic; on the west they flow to the Gulf of Mexico.

Take US 460 west of Blacksburg and Newport, turn right on County 700, and continue past the resort and the University of Virginia Biological Station, to where the road intersects with County 613. Follow County 613 to the War Spur parking lot. The Wind Rocks parking lot is three miles farther. Blacksburg Ranger District (703-552-4641).

Mount Rogers National Recreation Area — A 115,000-acre section of the Jefferson in Washington and Smyth Counties, this area was set aside especially for recreation. See heading in Chapter 1. Clinch Ranger District (703-328-2931).

Natural Bridge — In southern Rockbridge County, nearly surrounded by the Jefferson, is one of the Seven Natural Wonders of the World. Perhaps George Washington, who surveyed Natural Bridge and left his initials in its wall, and Thomas Jefferson, who owned it, knew the real meaning of the word *awesome* as they looked in amazement at this 215-foot-high limestone arch.

The stone span was carved out over the centuries by Cedar Creek on its way to the James River. The arch joins two mountains and supports the old Valley Pike, US 11. Natural Bridge Caverns are nearby. Privately owned. Natural Bridge, P.O. Box 57, Natural Bridge, VA 24578 (703-291-2121).

Roaring Run National Recreation Trail — In a gap in the Rich Patch Mountains south of Clifton Forge, the swift and powerful current of Roaring Run has gouged out a canyon with steep rock walls bordered by tall hemlocks and birches. The trail here is an easy, well-marked, one-and-a-half-mile loop, with steps in treacherous areas. The picnic area and trail are on County 621 in Botetourt County near the Alleghany County border. New Castle Ranger District (703-864-5195).

Seven Sisters Trail – This well-marked path in northern Wythe County provides a moderately difficult four-mile hike and a challenging course for mountain biking. Starting from the County 717 parking lot about one mile west of I-77, you'll climb from a bottomland of old-growth white pine to the top of Little Walker Mountain and continue along the ridge for several miles before coming down into the Stony Fork Campground and Dark Horse Hollow Picnic Area. The very popular East Fork of Stony Fork Creek is stocked for trout fishing and flows along part of the sixteen-mile Big Walker Mountain Scenic Byway on County 717. Wythe Ranger District (703-228-5551).

Shawvers Run Wilderness Area – To reach this 3,467-acre remote mountainous section of northwestern Craig County, take State 311 north from New Castle and turn right at the top of Potts Mountain on Forest Road 177-1. The wilderness area is three miles ahead on the left. Camping is available, and you can fish from turbulent trout-stocked Potts Creek at nearby Steel Bridge on State 18 north of Paint Bank. New Castle Ranger District (703-864-5195).

White Rocks Campground – Located in a wooded valley between Kire and Potts Mountains in Giles County, White Rocks provides access to the Appalachian Trail, Mountain Lake Wilderness Area, and Stony Creek and White Rocks Branch fishing areas. Go two miles west of Pembroke on US 460 and turn right on County 635. Continue seventeen miles to the campground. Blacksburg Ranger District (703-552-4641).

LAKE MOOMAW

It's a challenge these days to discover a public place of significant natural beauty that hasn't started showing signs of wear and tear.

There are so many of us trying to crowd into a limited number of places to camp, canoe, fish, and hike. In Virginia, which is within a day's drive of much of the heavily populated East Coast, the better-known public recreation areas such as Shenandoah National Park are beginning to resemble Disneyland on a summer weekend.

Ah, but we've found a delightful spot that hasn't been despoiled by crowds and overuse – not yet, anyway. If you hurry, you may get there before the rest of the world finds it.

The place is Lake Moomaw, named for the late Covington businessman Ben Moomaw, who championed the idea of a major flood-control and recreation lake in the mountains years before anyone else gave it serious consideration. This beautiful body of water – twelve miles long with forty-three miles of cove-studded shoreline – is set in the folds of the Alleghany Mountains near the West Virginia state line.

After spending several days and nights on the lake and prowling the mountains that surround it, we can tell you that the place is so stunningly beautiful that any description is as inadequate as a topo map of the Grand Canyon.

We were especially impressed with the variety of wildlife around the 2,530-acre lake. Fat groundhogs waddle across the road. From the forest comes the warbling song of the wood thrush, like water in a brook. Deer drift to the water's edge at twilight to drink, and waterfowl are abundant.

The U.S. Forest Service maintains campgrounds, swimming beaches, and picnic facilities at both the north and south ends of the lake. In Bath County on the north end, the Bolar Mountain area has three campgrounds, a swimming beach, hiking trails, a boat launch, two picnic areas, and a concession-operated marina and camp store.

Across the lake in Alleghany County is newly developed Coles Point Recreation Area, with a swimming beach, bathhouse, boat ramp, dock, hiking trail, and picnic shelters. Also

Raccoons enjoy picnics, too

on this side are campsites, two group shelters, and picnic tables at Cole Mountain and a boat ramp at Fortney Branch.

Check out the Gathright Dam Visitor Center to learn how engineering innovation was used to form a world-class trout fishery downstream of the dam. Much of the lake is bordered by the Gathright Wildlife Management Area and George Washington National Forest, with outstanding populations of deer, turkey, bear, and grouse.

Where: Western Alleghany and Bath Counties, seventeen miles north of Covington, close to West Virginia line.
Hours: Boat launches open all year. Campgrounds generally open May to October. Bathhouse at swimming beach from Memorial Day to Labor Day.
Admission: Day use parking fee. Campground fees (swimming included) are modest but vary per site, extra for reserved sites. Seasonal parking fee at boat ramps; annual use permit available.
Best time to visit: Avoid Memorial Day weekend, Fourth of July, and Labor Day weekend if you don't like crowds or if you don't have a campsite reservation. Otherwise, overcrowding is rare. Roads are not maintained in winter.
Activities: Freshwater fishing, boating (maximum of twenty-five feet), camping (some primitive sites; some with bathrooms, electricity, hot water), hiking, two swimming beaches with bathhouse (no lifeguard), picnicking (some areas have shelters, grills, rest rooms).
Concessions: Camp store at Bolar Flat.
Pets: Must be on leash.
For more information:

District Ranger, James River Ranger District, George Washington National Forest, 810-A Madison Avenue, Covington, VA 24426 (703-962-2214).

Warm Springs Ranger District, Route 2, Box 30, Hot Springs, VA 24445 (703-839-2521). For reservations, call

800-280-2267. Number for hearing- and speech-impaired, 800-879-4496.

MOUNT ROGERS NATIONAL RECREATION AREA

Some see it as a breathtaking blanket of Montana big sky country, draped across the flinty backbone of the Blue Ridge mountain range.

Perhaps. Nothing else in Virginia looks quite like Mount Rogers National Recreation Area. This is the roof of Virginia, with Mount Rogers, the highest peak in the state at 5,729 feet, and Whitetop Mountain, the second highest at 5,520 feet. Whitetop was named by early settlers who could see snow in the high country long after it had melted in the valleys.

In this lightly populated section of Virginia are great rock outcroppings thrust through the earth's surface. Expansive mountain "balds," or meadows, some going back to Native American times, dot the mountain slopes. Eighty miles of clear streams — cold and pure enough for both stocked rainbow trout and native brook trout, or char — cascade through hemlock-shaded hollows. Forested mountain ranges, bunched like the folds in an old blue quilt, spread all the way into North Carolina and Tennessee.

Rare Species

A place so high in the clouds, so often drenched in mist and cloaked in fog, so different from the rest of the state is bound to be home to flora and fauna peculiar to the area. For example, there are rare species of salamanders beneath the rocks and in the creeks of Mount Rogers. Red spruce is more common to Canada and New England, but the dark evergreen is scattered throughout the high country of these protected forests. The spruce emerged after the last ice age some 10,000 years ago.

On a high peak, a friend once pointed out the curious and mischievous red squirrels scampering through the hickories and hemlocks. They're only half as big as the common gray squirrel. These red squirrels don't care for Virginia's low country, and are found only at the highest elevations. Local people call them "boomers."

This is Virginia at its most beautiful. In fact, there are three pristine areas with a wilderness designation here—Lewis Fork, Little Wilson Creek, and Little Dry Run. You would expect that where good roads access such grandeur, locating an available campsite might be difficult in the summer, especially if you've experienced the crowds in, say, Claytor Lake State Park.

Not so. Even in midsummer at Mount Rogers, the six established campgrounds—all near good trout streams—are usually uncrowded. We've found that if we can live without electric and water hookups (this recreation area doesn't have them yet), we're much more apt to find a campsite most anywhere, even in peak season. Three of the campgrounds do have hot showers. There's a certain freedom in knowing, too, that you can unroll a sleeping bag anywhere in the area to rest your head. (This is true in all of Virginia's national forests and wilderness areas.)

Located just east of the intersection of County 603 and Forest Route 828 in the heart of the Mount Rogers national recreation area is the largest campground, Grindstone, with 100 campsites and an unusual water playground for children, created with a diverted mountain stream.

It's just a short hike—and well worth the trouble—from the campground to the Mount Rogers Trail and into Lewis Fork Wilderness. There you can experience firsthand a place that, as described in the Wilderness Act that protects it, "generally appears to have been affected primarily by the forces of nature, with the imprint of man's work substantially unnoticeable. . . ."

Remember, especially in wilderness areas, to carry out

whatever you carry in, leaving only footprints behind. It's called "no-trace ethics"—a good practice in all outdoor preserves.

Hiking Trails

Whether you have just an hour or less to take a little loop trail or time to do some serious exploring, the recreation area has something for all outdoor lovers. There are 400 miles of trails covering all kinds of terrain and all degrees of difficulty—such a smorgasbord, in fact, it's hard to know where to start.

Cross-country skiers take advantage of the less rugged trails and the gorgeous scenery in winter. Mountain biking is allowed on all trails except the Appalachian Trail, trails designated for hikers only, and trails within wilderness areas.

About 54 miles of the Appalachian Trail, which runs from Georgia to Maine, meanders through Mount Rogers, snaking into and out of wilderness areas along spruce-fir ridges, down into rhododendron-laced hollows, over cascading streams, and back up into the rarefied air of windswept buttes, reminiscent of scenery from an old Rocky Lane shoot-'em-up.

About half of the Virginia Creeper Trail, which lies along an abandoned railroad bed between the North Carolina border and Abingdon, Virginia, is within the national recreation area. Hikers, horseback riders, and bicyclists share the trail. (See heading in Chapter 1.)

At the visitors center on State 16 south of Marion, helpful Mount Rogers interpretive specialist Bob McKinney answered our questions and directed us to a good trout-fishing stream. At the visitors center, we picked up an excellent water-resistant topographic map and guide entitled "Mount Rogers High Country and Wildernesses." The guide has information on campground facilities, and trail locations, distances, and difficulty. Other helpful pamphlets and maps are available, many of them free, along with a selection of nature guides for sale. If half the family is waiting impatiently in the car, there's a nature trail right behind the visitors center that leads to two fishing ponds.

Horse Trails

Anyone who enjoys horseback riding on mountain trails is welcome on some 200 miles of orange-blazed trails in Mount Rogers—all but the white-blazed Appalachian Trail and a few other trails clearly marked for hikers only. The Virginia Highlands Horse Trail (orange diamond blazes) stretches sixty-seven miles from County 600 at Elk Garden Gap near Whitetop Mountain to State 94 near Ivanhoe and Raketown. The trail passes close to the summit of Mount Rogers and skirts the edge of beautiful Grayson Highlands State Park, where you can take a side trail to a campground and stable in the park (fees apply).

There are also three primitive campgrounds for equestrians at Fox Creek, Hussy Mountain, and Raven Cliff, with hitching posts and parking for horse trailers.

Horseback trips and mule-drawn covered-wagon trips are offered from May 1 to October 1 by a concessionaire, the Mount Rogers High Country Outdoor Center. The livery is located at Fairwood, an old Grayson County logging community about four miles west of Trout Dale on State 603. There are several trips to choose from, but the most popular is a four-mile ride to an altitude of 4,600 feet at a place called the Scales, where the high country begins. An overnight wagon or horseback trip, complete with pack mules, is also available. All meals, tents, and equipment, except sleeping bags, are provided.

The Virginia Department of Game and Inland Fisheries stocks rainbow trout in about fifty miles of streams and two lakes. Because of water purity and the voluntary catch-and-release policy that promotes good native fish populations, fishing for rainbow, brown, and brook trout is available on an additional fifty miles of streams.

Where: Between Marion and North Carolina border in southwestern Virginia. From I-81, exit 45, at Marion, take State 16 south seven miles.

Hours: Always open. Some campgrounds seasonal.

Admission: No admission charge. Livery fees for horseback, wagon trips.

Best time to visit: Anytime for trail use. June 10 to 15 for rhododendron bloom. Late September to early October for fall foliage.

Activities: Hiking, mountain biking, horseback riding, cross-country skiing, camping, wildlife and nature observation, scenic drives, interpretive trails, trout fishing, mule-drawn wagon trips.

Concessions: Horseback and covered-wagon trips.

Pets: Must be on leash.

Other: Whitetop Mountain Maple Festival in March, Mount Rogers Ramp Festival in May, Galax Old Fiddlers Convention in early August, Grayson Highlands Fall Festival in late September.

Fox Hill Inn bed and breakfast south of Trout Dale (800-874-3313). Marion has motels and restaurants.

For more information:

Area Ranger, Mount Rogers National Recreation Area, U.S. Forest Service, Route 1, Box 303, Marion, VA 24354 (703-783-5196).

Mount Rogers High Country Outdoor Center, P.O. Box 151, Trout Dale, VA 24378-0151 (703-677-3900).

NATURAL TUNNEL STATE PARK

Around 1880, about 100 years after Daniel Boone is supposed to have stood on the rim and looked far down at Natural Tunnel,

William Jennings Bryan strode to the edge and declared this gigantic hole through the mountain to be "the eighth wonder of the world."

They didn't call him Bombastic Bryan for nothing.

But Natural Tunnel doesn't need that kind of exaggerated endorsement. True, it took more than a million years for a cascading creek to gouge this 850-foot-long chute through what appears to be solid stone. And true, the immensity of nature's work is intimidating when you stand at the bottom of the fossil-embedded limestone basin 400 feet below the rim and see the tunnel swallow one of the loaded coal trains that creep through it daily. But the tunnel and the beautiful mountain park that surround it can stand on their own merits.

In spring, wildflowers such as columbine, jack-in-the-pulpit, and fire pink dress the hills with pastel color. As summer approaches, leaves of tulip poplar and American beech shade the forest floor. In autumn, each tree contributes a patchwork of brilliant fall color as it prepares for winter dormancy.

The place is steeped in history. Much of the eastern pioneer migration to the Ohio and Mississippi River regions and beyond passed close by. At nearby Big Stone Gap, the long-running outdoor drama *The Trail of the Lonesome Pine* retells the frontier story each June, July, and August.

During the Civil War, Confederate troops mined saltpeter (potassium nitrate) in the tunnel, for gunpowder and explosives. And this park is near the edge of the Appalachian coalfields of Virginia and Kentucky. A coal museum is also in Big Stone Gap.

But everything isn't a hundred years old.

An exciting 536-foot-long ride on a new cable-operated chairlift carries visitors 230 feet down to the canyon floor and the mouth of the tunnel. An interpreter explains how the water carved the tunnel out of limestone rock.

The best views of Natural Tunnel have been made wheelchair accessible. The chairlift to the canyon floor connects to a boardwalk that leads to the mouth of the tunnel; another board-walk, 500 feet long, leads to an observation deck above the tunnel.

By the time you visit, the planned environmental education center may also be completed.

We recommend the half-mile Lover's Leap Trail over the rim high above the tunnel. You can pick up a brochure at the visitors center to help interpret the trail and explain the legend behind the name. The longest of the five hiking trails here is less than a mile.

Because this park is not located close to any large population areas, it is rarely crowded. The addition of electric and water hookups for the campgrounds may make it more attractive to overnighters, but it will probably still be less crowded than most parks, even during the busy season.

Where: Scott County, in southwestern Virginia. From Gate City, take US 23 north about thirteen miles, then go one mile east on County 871.

Hours: Hiking trails 8:00 A.M. until dusk daily, year-round. Chairlift, swimming, visitors center, interpretive programs, Memorial Day weekend to Labor Day. Chairlift also operates weekends-only in spring and fall. Campgrounds open spring through fall. Check park for exact dates.

Admission: Small parking and chairlift fees.

Best time to visit: Anytime for hiking, viewing tunnel. Spring through fall for chairlift, camping. Summer for swimming.

Activities: Hiking or riding chairlift to view Natural Tunnel, camping (some hookups available), modern swimming complex, large shaded picnic area with grills, visitors center, amphitheater, interpretive programs, stocked trout fishing.

Concessions: Chairlift. Food concession in pool area.

Pets: Must be on leash.

For more information:
Natural Tunnel State Park, Route 3, Box 250, Duffield, VA
24244 (703-940-2674 or 804-786-1712).

NEW RIVER TRAIL STATE PARK

Rivers are mysterious. They play tag with our highways, then
wander off on their own, leaving us to wonder if they'll reappear.

Some of us feel a strong urge to trace the twists and turns of
every shining ribbon of water, to follow the river's hidden journey through mountain passes and beyond.

If you've ever had a Huck Finn kind of itch to know where
a river is going or where it has been, you'll love the fifty-seven-
mile stretch of old railroad bed that is New River Trail State
Park.

This is a long, skinny park. Planners call it "linear." Hug-
ging the banks of the ancient New River and Chestnut Creek, the
park winds through the rural counties of Grayson, Carroll,
Wythe, and Pulaski. Thirty-seven miles of trail in the park have
been opened to the public. A twenty-mile stretch between the
I-77 bridge in Wythe County to Allisonia in Pulaski County is
still under development.

The New River got its name during Colonial times, when
southwestern Virginia was called New Virginia. But, in truth,
the age of the river is estimated at 350 million years—making it
one of the oldest rivers in the world. It is one of the few rivers in
North America that flow north.

The railroad—originally called the Cripple Creek line—was
built in the late 1800s to carry iron and lead from area mines to
industrial centers. As the mines played out, the Norfolk Southern
Corporation abandoned the railroad and donated the right-of-way
to the state Department of Conservation and Recreation. Rem-
nants of the old mines are still evident.

The trail features two tunnels to walk through, three major bridges, and nearly thirty smaller bridges and trestles. You can see a good deal of wildlife. There are heart-shaped deer tracks in the soft cinders, and a fat groundhog is likely to peep over the bank as you pass. We also watched kingfishers dive for minnows in the river alongside the trail. Bass chased smaller fish below the riffles, ducks drifted in the shade of the willows near the shore, and two red-tailed hawks pierced the autumn afternoon with their sharp, whistling cries.

Plan to share the trail with cyclists, horses, and other walkers. Except for weekends in summer, it won't be overly crowded, but walkers complain that bikers in particular don't always ring a bell or shout a warning when they're bearing down. Where wooden walkways replaced the old railroad, trail users can expect to walk across beautiful restored trestles and bridges.

The New River Trail also provides access for canoeing, kayaking, and fishing. Order a free map (see below) for access points and features along the way.

Here are just a few of many interesting mileposts.

Milepost 8   Delton Trestle

Milepost 19.6   Bertha Cave (bats live here)

Milepost 24   Foster Falls

Milepost 25.3   Shot Tower

Milepost 29   Austinville lead mines

Milepost 38.6   Old-time spa

Milepost 40.1   Site of 1928 train wreck

Milepost 40.6   Chestnut Tunnel, 195 feet long

Milepost 41.5   Sign of beaver activity

Milepost 45   Company houses

Milepost 45.1   Train turntable

Trail parking areas are at the following places: Town of Galax (where US 58 crosses Chestnut Creek). In Carroll County, at Cliffview (north of Galax, where County 721 crosses Chestnut Creek), Gambetta and Chestnut Yard (north on County 721 past

RAILS TO TRAILS

You don't get many opportunities to travel the serpentine path of a river, because landowners have erected fences to keep you out. But with the passing of the railroad as a mode of transportation, hiking and biking enthusiasts began to realize the potential for trails in the old, abandoned railroad beds.

Railroad companies are often glad to donate their property for a new use. The beds are perfect for hiking, bicycling, and horseback riding. They follow rivers, byways, and mountain ranges through beautiful and remote countryside. As a bonus, the railroad beds are relatively level.

Ironically, what was once the path of the great locomotives that powered the industrial revolution is now the path of the oldest mode of travel known to man—foot power.

One problem that park departments and other trail developers have encountered is the reluctance of property owners to allow trail users to hike through. The manager of the New River Trail says the fears have been unfounded. So far, hikers, bicyclists, and horseback riders have been good stewards of the trail and respectful of adjacent landowners.

Cliffview), Byllesby Dam, and Buck Dam. In Wythe County, at Austinville and at Shot Tower Historical State Park (administrative office). In Pulaski County, at Draper and Pulaski/Xaloy.

The trail may also be accessed at Hiwasee, Allisonia, Ivanhoe, Lone Ash, Barren Spring, and Fries, though there are no developed parking areas at these entrances.

Horse trailers may be parked at the Cliffview, Draper, and Shot Tower entrances only.

Parking for persons with disabilities is available at the Ivanhoe and Cliffview entrances, with rest rooms at Cliffview.

Unless you're near Shot Tower or Cliffview, currently the only locations with water fountains, better carry your own water.

Where: Southwestern Virginia, from Fries in Grayson County north along New River fifty-seven miles to Pulaski.
Hours: 8:00 A.M. until dark daily, year-round.
Admission: No fee.
Best time to visit: Spring, fall, winter. Trail traffic can be heavy in summer, especially on Sundays.
Activities: Hiking, bicycling, horseback riding, picnicking, wildlife observation, fishing, canoeing, kayaking.
Concessions: Convenience stores in Draper, on County 721 near Fries, in Galax, approximately half a mile off trail in Austinville, and on State 94 in Ivanhoe.
Pets: Must be on leash.
Other: Town park at Fries, Mount Rogers National Recreation Area, Shot Tower Historical State Park, boat launches at Fries and north of Allisonia.
For more information:
    New River Trail State Park, Route 1, Box 81X, Austinville, VA 24312 (703-699-6778 or 804-786-1712).

PINNACLE NATURAL AREA PRESERVE

Perhaps it happened this way. . . .
    In some bubbling cauldron eons ago, a wizard tossed a little limestone, dolomite, and sandstone. Satisfied, he poured his strange brew out over Copper Ridge in what is now Russell County, where it sank into bedrock.
    There, the mixture simmered through the centuries, endlessly washed by the gurgling southwestern Virginia waters of Big Cedar Creek and the meandering Clinch River, purified by falling rains. The concoction lay dormant, exposed to the effects of weather and time.
    What emerged in this little corner of Virginia was, in its own way, unlike any other place on earth. At first glance,

whatever happened here may not impress today's Jurassic Park generation, zeroed in on gargantuan size and lots of action. Rather, unique genetic combinations found fertile soil in which to grow, like the solution to some strange theorem. A hodge-podge of seeds and pollen were blown in on the wind, transported inside a bird's crop or carried piggyback on an animal's fur. Delicate wildflowers and lacy ferns came to love the rich dolomite and limestone ledges. Smooth cliff-brake, Carey's saxifrage, and glade spurge grew here. The forces of wind and water carved out strange and wondrous rock formations and towering cliffs.

In the Clinch River, the birdwing pearly mussel – known to exist in just one other river on earth – found a home. The spiny riversnail, the soft-shell turtle, and the hellbender also made a pact with the river for survival.

With donated land from Russell County and assistance from The Nature Conservancy, the Pinnacle Natural Area Preserve was set aside by the Virginia Department of Conservation and Recreation to protect twelve of these rare plant species, nine rare animal species, and two rare natural communities.

The first objective in setting aside such natural areas is protection. As a result, many areas do not have developed public access. Pinnacle Natural Area, however, has a trail system built by the Young Adult Conservation Corps in 1978.

At the end of the parking area beside the Big Falls picnic shelter, follow the trail along the bank of Big Cedar Creek through rich cove woodlands. Then climb through a ridgetop glade of rare wildflowers, including the American harebell, tufted hairgrass, Canby's mountain lover, and white camas.

Even if you don't know tufted hairgrass from rabbit tobacco, there's still plenty to enjoy here. The most obvious is the view from the trail summit on Copper Ridge. Glinting in the sun below are the cascading waters of Big Cedar Creek heading for the Clinch River. Rising an impressive 600 feet above Big Cedar is a dolomite rock formation—the Pinnacle.

Explore the fragile environment of the preserve to your heart's content, being careful to stay on the trails to avoid trampling any insignificant-looking but perhaps rare plant.

Before making a trip to Pinnacle Natural Area Preserve, we suggest talking with the helpful rangers at Hungry Mother State Park, which administers the preserve, to find out what unusual wildflowers are in bloom.

While you're in the area, consider a visit to beautiful Hidden Valley Lake, located high atop Brumley Mountain in the Jefferson National Forest just a few miles south of Lebanon. The steep road up the mountain may be treacherous in winter. From US 19, take County 690 to the top.

Where: Russell County, seven miles northeast of Lebanon. Take State 82 north a short distance to County 640. Go right on County 640 four miles and left on a gravel road, County 721, to parking lot.

Hours: Open daily sunrise to sunset, year-round.

Admission: No charge.

Best time to visit: Anytime, except when high water, ice, or snow may block gravel entrance road.

Activities: Hiking, swimming, scenic views, nature study, fishing, picnicking.

Concessions: None.

Pets: Must be on leash.

For more information:

Hungry Mother State Park, Route 5, Box 109, Marion, VA 24354 (703-783-3422 or 804-786-1712).

SKY MEADOWS STATE PARK

Sky Meadows is an outdoor-lover's park: a place for those who find their recreation in watching the courtship flight of a pair of woodcock at twilight; a place for quiet woodland walks; a place where a field guide and a spreading field of wildflowers take precedence over a Ludlum novel and a beach.

Despite its unusual beauty, Sky Meadows doesn't boast the facilities that attract crowds in some of the more fully developed parks.

For example, the twelve campsites are primitive, with pit toilets and nonpotable water. To get to them, you have to hike three-quarters of a mile from the visitors center. There is no lake stretching for miles for roaring bassboats, no lifeguarded swimming beach, and no water slides.

But there is country serenity and gentleness in the mountain scenery. And there's a little farm pond where you can bring the children to catch some perch and bluegill. There's even an eleven-stall barn with corral for campers with horses, and more than five miles of challenging, picturesque bridle trails.

The name Sky Meadows is in keeping with this pastoral setting, where the rolling hills of the Piedmont rise to meet the mountains in northern Virginia.

Early in spring, the purple blooms of the redbud tree and the white dogwood blossoms paint a gay palette over winter's drab remains. Soon the high meadows run right up to the sky with a fresh crop of daisies, and the woods are spiced with wild columbine, fire pink, lady's slipper, and trillium.

Summer brings many hikers off the Appalachian Trail, glad to find a place of such solitude to put up a tent. With its three-mile section of the Appalachian Trail, Sky Meadow is one of the few places in the area to provide public access to the Trail. After miles of rugged mountain ridges, hikers are eager to explore the high open pastures and grassy slopes of the park.

Old fencerows made of stone were carefully fitted and stacked here to endure through the generations. In October, the reds and ochres on the hillsides are brilliant against the neutral background of the stone fences.

In keeping with the concept of the 1,900-acre park, the

A trillium

visitors center is located in an antebellum farmhouse, the Mount
Bleak House, restored with period furniture. The park's rich history is illustrated here, in part through the diary of a young girl
who once lived on the property. You can also learn about a

former owner, George M. Slater, a Confederate soldier who first saw the area while serving as one of Mosby's Rangers, and who came back after the war to live here for some fifty-five years.

For hunting, fishing, and some of the best wildflower displays in the state, visit the high woodlands of the G. Richard Thompson Wildlife Management Area, adjacent to the park and managed by the Virginia Department of Game and Inland Fisheries.

Late April to mid-May is the best time to see forests full of trillium in the wildlife area. Naturalists, botanists, and sightseers alike gaze open-mouthed at the astonishing display of delicate three-petaled wildflowers carpeting the forest floor in white, pink, fuchsia, and maroon.

Writing in *Virginia Wildlife* magazine, Nancy Hugo says, "You can walk for hours on the trails that wind through the upper reaches of the Thompson and never be out of sight of trillium spreading as far as the eye can see." One botanist, figuring the number of flowers per square yard, conservatively estimated the number in bloom at 18 million.

Timing is critical to seeing the trillium at the peak of bloom, which varies a little from year to year. One year we arrived a week too late and could only look sadly at the dead and drooping blooms of what had been, the week before, a sight to dazzle. Since then, we've found a friend in northern Virginia who keeps us posted. Lacking that, check with the park personnel for advice on when to go and where the best viewing spots are.

Where: Blue Ridge Mountains of Fauquier County, northeast of Front Royal, two miles south of Paris. From US 66, take US 17 (exit five) north seven miles. Park entrance is at County 710.
Hours: 8:00 A.M. until dusk daily, year-round.
Admission: Small parking fee.
Best time to visit: Spring through fall for interpretive programs, spring for wildflowers, anytime for hiking.

Activities: Hike-in primitive camping, bridle trails, picnicking (including shelters, drinking water, grills, rest room), hiking, self-guided trails, seasonal visitors center, environmental education center, interpretive programs including wildflower hikes, bird walks, astronomy, demonstrations of Civil War encampments.
Concessions: Vending machines.
Pets: Must be on leash.
For more information:
    Sky Meadows State Park, Route 1, Box 540, Delaplane, VA 22025-9508 (703-592-3556 or 804-786-1712).

SMITH MOUNTAIN LAKE STATE PARK

Members of the 1964 study commission that decided where to put a state park on sprawling Smith Mountain Lake deserve a medal. By strategically locating the new facility on a jutting peninsula full of coves, they built a park that has an impressive sixteen miles of shoreline on only 1,506 acres.

    Across the shining lake to the southeast, catching the sun's gold at evening, is prominent Smith Mountain, which gave the lake and park their names.

    To create this second-largest body of freshwater in Virginia, the Roanoke River was dammed in 1960 as a power source, backing up 20,000 acres of water. The lake quickly gained a reputation among recreation seekers as the place to go on a summer afternoon. Marinas, tackle shops, restaurants, and motels sprang up. Fishing guides passed out business cards. Today Smith Mountain Lake has more boat traffic in summer than almost any other body of water in the state.

    The lake's reputation for outdoor recreation is enhanced by the annual stocking by the Virginia Department of Game and Inland Fisheries of muskie, walleye, and striped bass. Anglers come from as far as Richmond and Virginia Beach to fish for the stocked fish, along with the lake's largemouth and smallmouth bass and pike. Fishing tournaments are a frequent draw.

The 500-foot swimming beach in the park is the only public swimming area on Smith Mountain Lake. At any one time on a sweltering July weekend, you might count as many as 1,000 people cooling themselves in the lake's waters.

With just fifty primitive campsites (for tents and trailers) and a cold-water shower, Smith Mountain State Park may seem to include camping only as an afterthought. However, with recent new funding, hookups will be added, along with furnished housekeeping cabins, an environmental education center, and improved boat access.

Park interpreters teach wilderness skills, conduct twilight programs, and take visitors on guided canoe trips and night hikes. You can pick up a booklet for the self-guided Turtle Island Trail, a loop trail designed to show the succession of growth from cleared fields to a mature beech, oak, and hickory forest.

Where: North shore of Smith Mountain Lake in Bedford County, about thirty-five miles east of Roanoke. Take State 24 from Roanoke (or US 460 from Lynchburg) to State 43 south to County 626 south to the park.

Hours: 8:00 a.m until dusk daily, year-round.

Admission: Small parking fee. Swimming, camping, boat-launching fees.

Best time to visit: Anytime for hiking and fishing, spring through fall for camping, summer for water activities.

Activities: Swimming beach, boat-launching ramp (motorboats permitted), waterskiing, fishing, hiking, camping, picnicking, visitors center, interpretive programs, amphitheater.

Concessions: Food concession at swimming complex, paddle-boat and rowboat rental.

Pets: Must be on leash.

Other: Smith Mountain Ruritans Bass Fishing Tournament in

March, Aspiring Anglers Junior Fishing Tournament in June, Smith Mountain Lake Triathlon in July, Smith Mountain Ruritan/ Cystic Fibrosis Bikathon in October. Motels and private campgrounds plentiful around lake.

For more information:

Smith Mountain Lake State Park, Route 1, Box 41, Huddleston, VA 24104-9547 (703-297-6066 or 804-786-1712).

VIRGINIA CREEPER TRAIL

In her marvelous book *A Natural History of the Senses* Diane Ackerman says that memory and the sense of smell are "tightly coupled."

True, true. Certain aromas have the power to enhance reality, to transport us to another place and time.

When that happens, we may be—suddenly, pleasantly, miraculously—ten years old again, picking bright-red straw-·berries beside shimmering railroad tracks with a grandmother who believes her world took substance and form only after we arrived on the scene.

That's just what happened on the Virginia Creeper Trail, one of Virginia's more unusual trails for hiking, biking, horseback riding, and cross-country skiing. The smooth, cinder-covered path begins in Abingdon and concludes some thirty-three miles away in the mountains at the North Carolina line.

Within the first quarter mile after we began our hike one day in early fall, a familiar aroma wafted up from the ground. It was the oily, emotion-laden odor of train smoke that we remembered from childhood. Pungent black train smoke permeates, even colors, the soil of the Creeper trail, even after 100 years.

There aren't many things in this world that smell as good as train smoke. And there aren't many trails that we'd rather walk than the Virginia Creeper.

Part of it is the history. The Virginia Creeper Trail is named for steam engine number 433. The old black engine is now parked at the entrance of the trail inside the city limits of Abingdon. For more than three-quarters of a century, the coal-burning steam engine chugged its way back and forth between Abingdon, Virginia, and Elkland, North Carolina, hauling timber, iron ore, supplies for mountain communities, and passengers.

Because it was so slow, the train was lovingly called the Virginia Creeper. After all, it had to cross White Top Mountain, the second-highest point in Virginia, as well as 100 trestles across rivers and gorges in some of the most forbidding terrain in the state.

Abingdon is a restored frontier town—the first English-speaking town on waters flowing to the Mississippi River. Three Virginia governors lived here. The first post office in the southwestern part of frontier Virginia was established in Abingdon in 1793.

The Virginia Creeper Trail was originally a Native American trail, then a railroad, now once again an outdoor seeker's footpath. It is one of the finest examples of a fledgling national effort to convert abandoned railway beds to hiking and biking trails.

This hiker's dream, however, has enough interesting features to stand alone, even if it were built somewhere else and had no past that included Native Americans, frontier settlers, loggers, steam engines, and almost certainly a moonshiner or two. The trail (never more than a 6 percent grade) passes under I-81 with its snarling tractor trailers and its whining automobile traffic; through Glenroachie Country Club golf course; across a series of valleys and ridges called the Great Knobs beside Holston and Iron Mountains; and past the communities of Watauga, Alvarado, and Damascus.

You'll gradually climb past several Daniel Boone campsites and beaver dams, cross river trestles that span trout and smallmouth bass streams pouring out of the mountains toward the Mississippi, and end up near White Top Station at the North Carolina line deep in the Blue Ridge range.

What a train ride that must have been. What a walk or a bike ride it is today.

Rental bikes are available in Abingdon at Highland Ski and Outdoor Center. Parking and access areas along the length of the trail make entry and exit easy. Consider getting on a bike at a high elevation and gently coasting down to Abingdon.

Parking is available at the Abingdon Trailhead, mile 0; County 677, mile 2.9; Alvarado, mile 8.5; Damascus, mile 15.5; Straight Branch, mile 19.5; Taylor's Valley, mile 21; Konnarock Junction, mile 24; Green Cove Station, mile 29.3, and Whitetop Station, mile 32.3.

Take water, a snack, and warm clothing. The weather can change dramatically in the high country.

Where: From Abingdon, VA, running thirty-three miles southeast past Damascus to Virginia–North Carolina line.

Hours: Always open.

Admission: No charge.

Best time to visit: Anytime. Weekdays are less crowded.

Activities: Hiking, bicycling, horseback riding, wildlife observation, camping (no established campsites; camp well off trail, and camp on private property only with permission).

Concessions: Mile 21, Taylor's Valley, snacks.

Pets: Leash highly recommended; required on U.S. Forest Service property.

For more information:

Virginia Creeper Trail Club, P.O. Box 2382, Abingdon, VA 24210.

Mount Rogers National Recreation Area, Route 1, Box 303, Marion, VA 24354 (703-783-5196).

2

Central Region (Piedmont)

BUGGS ISLAND LAKE (KERR RESERVOIR) AND LAKE GASTON

Buggs Island Lake and Lake Gaston, two major impoundments shared by Virginia and North Carolina, are natural magnets to those who love boating, fishing, waterskiing, camping, and related activities.

If you're a Virginian, the major lake is called Buggs Island. If you're a North Carolinian, it's Kerr Reservoir. (There's no argument about Lake Gaston.) The reasons for disputing the name are complex and not very important—no more important, say, than the reasons Virginians call themselves Cavaliers and Carolinians refer to themselves as Tarheels.

The John H. Kerr dam, where State 4 crosses the lake southeast of Boydton, backs the sprawling, 50,000-acre Buggs Island Lake thirty-nine miles up the Roanoke River. Hundreds of picturesque coves make up 800 miles of wooded shoreline.

Lake Gaston stretches for thirty-four miles from the John H. Kerr dam at Buggs Island Lake southeast to the Gaston Dam west of I-95 and Roanoke Rapids, North Carolina. This North Carolina Power facility covers 20,300 acres and has more than 340 miles of shoreline. Most of Buggs Island Lake is in Virginia, while most of Lake Gaston lies in North Carolina. Both Buggs Island and Gaston are famous for the number and size of their fish, especially largemouth bass, striped bass, and crappie. Fishing is also good for bluegill, perch, and walleye. Several state and regional fishing tournaments are held on the lakes annually.

Occoneechee State Park and Staunton River State Park

The two state parks at Buggs Island attract hundreds of thousands of visitors annually. Though they are just nine miles apart as the crow flies, Occoneechee State Park and Staunton River State Park are separated by the Roanoke River, and driving between them takes forty-five minutes.

Water activities are the focus of area recreation, but there are other attractions, too.

The three miles of wooded trails on the northern end of Occoneechee offer a history lesson in plantation life of the 1800s and a study of the Occoneechee Native Americans, who lived on a nearby island from 1250 to 1670. The park takes its name from the once-dominant tribe. Shaded campsites at the water's edge allow visitors today to camp where the Occoneechees once built their fires.

The Occoneechee tribe attained a high state of culture. By fortifying the bluffs along the Roanoke River, they dominated the area for some 400 years, until Nathaniel Bacon stormed their village, stole an impressive cache of furs, and killed their king in 1676.

For an enjoyable side trip, visit Prestwould Plantation, just

THE LOON

Camped in a tent beside the water at Occoneechee State Park one night some twenty years ago, we were almost asleep when a wild yodeling echoed across the dark water. We snapped upright in our sleeping bags.

"A loon," she exclaimed, though our limited knowledge of the loon's wild call came more from movies than from good field detective work.

"Can't be," he said with the authority of one who bluffs when he isn't sure. "There are no loons in Virginia."

Still, we went to sleep with the sound of those mournful calls drifting from somewhere out on the big lake. As a result, the first thing we did when we got home was slap the record of Peterson's "A Field Guide to Bird Songs" on the record player. There it was—not someone's practical joke at all. We had indeed heard a common loon on a Virginia lake.

Subsequent prowling through field guides assured us that loons do come south through Virginia, and we've since seen and heard them from the coast inland. The quavering cry of a loon—like geese across a full moon or the howl of a wolf—bespeaks wildness.

Loon numbers appear to have increased since that camping trip twenty years ago. You may hear loons calling now at Buggs Island Lake or at any of several other places in eastern and southeastern Virginia, especially near the coast.

A small goose-sized bird floating low, showing only a glossy black head and neck with white collar, is probably a loon. Few other birds this size swim so low in the water that they appear to be waterlogged.

---

three miles northwest of Occoneechee State Park on US 15. Built in 1795 by Sir Peyton Skipwith, the manor house is notable especially for its scenic wallpapers and library. The house and gardens are open to the public from May to September.

At the peninsular tip of Occoneechee State Park is a wildlife management area with four additional miles of hiking trails and access for hunters. Contact the park office for hunting regulations.

The second park on Buggs Island Lake, Staunton River State Park, is a good place to bring the family. The park features camping, swimming and wading pools, tennis courts, boat rental, and cabins.

Many facilities are soon to be upgraded and renovated, including the pool and tennis courts. To be sure that the pool and courts are open, call ahead. Installation of water and electric hookups for camping and the addition of heat and air-conditioning to the cabins are also on the "to do" list.

Where: Occoneechee State Park, near Clarksville, 1.5 miles east on US 58 near US 15 intersection. Staunton River State Park, eighteen miles east of South Boston; take US 360 north, then State 344 east ten miles.

Hours: Hiking, picnicking, boat ramps 8:00 A.M. until dusk daily, year-round. Camping, interpretive programs seasonal.

Admission: Small parking fee. Boat-launch and camping fees. Pool fee and cabin rental fee at Staunton River.

Best time to visit: Warm weather for water activities. Off-season for hiking, picnicking. Group facilities reserved weeks in advance during summer.

Activities: Excellent fishing in lakes. Occoneechee has freshwater fishing, two boat ramps (motorboats permitted), paddleboat and johnboat rental, campsites (electric hookup available), lakefront picnic areas with shelters, amphitheater, interpretive programs, hiking trails, several new bathhouses. Staunton River has freshwater fishing, boat launching (motorboats permitted), rowboat, canoe and paddleboat rental, camping, group camping, picnic areas, housekeeping cabins, hiking, self-guided trails, swimming and wading pools, tennis courts, visitors center, interpretive programs, some wheelchair access.

Concessions: Occoneechee, grocery store and vending machines; Staunton River, grocery store and snack bar.

Pets: Must be on leash. Not allowed in pool area at Staunton River.

Other: Seaplanes allowed on Buggs Island Lake. Contact Corps of Engineers for details.

For more information:

Occoneechee State Park, P.O. Box 3, Clarksville, VA 23927 (804-374-2210 or 804-786-1712).

Staunton River State Park, Route 2, Box 295, Scottsburg, VA 24589 (804-572-4623 or 804-786-1712).

Public Recreation Areas

The Corps of Engineers operates many public recreation areas and campgrounds on Buggs Island Lake in Virginia and North Carolina. Most of the day-use areas have a beach, swimming area, launch ramp, and picnic tables (some with pavilions); most have a small day-user fee.

The Corps campgrounds are generally open May to September, charging a small fee for day use and a modest fee for campsites with hookups. Off-season camping is available free (small charge for campsites with hookups) at North Bend, Longwood, and Rudds Creek parks.

The most complete recreation area is North Bend Park and Marina, just north of the dam and west of State 4. Facilities here include 246 campsites (89 with water and electric hookups), hot showers, flush toilets, three boat ramps, an amphitheater, a small nature center, three swimming beaches, and a fishing pier with wheelchair access. Group camping facilities and programs are also available by reservation.

Newly renovated Rudds Creek Recreation Area near Boydton has 100 sites (most with water and electric hookups), hot showers, flush toilets, two boat ramps, an amphitheater, and swimming beach.

Longwood Park, just south of Clarksville, has fifty-five

tent or trailer campsites (eleven with hookups), flush toilets, boat ramp, hot showers, picnic area, and beach. Contact the Corps of Engineers for information about more campgrounds and recreation areas.

The first five-mile leg of a new historic hiking trail, the Robert Mumford Trail, has recently been opened by the Corps at Eagle Point, about seven miles south of Boydton. The trail winds back to the grave of this Revolutionary War soldier.

The town of Clarksville, located on the south side of the lake on US 15 and US 58, is well equipped to assist lake users. There you can find lodging, restaurants, grocery stores, laundromats, and a place to get fishing and hunting supplies and licenses.

North Carolina Power does not operate public recreation areas on Lake Gaston, but there is a private full-service campground (Americamps Lake Gaston, five miles southeast of I-85 and Bracey off County 903) and several boat-launching ramps on the Virginia shore of the lake.

Hours: 7:00 A.M. or 8:00 A.M. until dark, year-round, for day-use areas. May to September for most Buggs Island campgrounds (North Bend, Longwood, and Rudds Creek parks offer off-season camping). Year-round, Americamps Lake Gaston.
Admission: Small day-user fee. No admission charge October to April.
Best time to visit: Warm weather for water activities. Off-season for hiking and picnicking. Group facilities reserved weeks in advance during summer.
Activities: Beach, swimming area, picnicking, boat ramp at most areas; campgrounds, interpretive programs at some areas.
Concessions: None.
Pets: Must be on leash. Not allowed in swim areas.
For more information:
     North Bend (804-738-6143), Longwood (804-374-2711), Rudds Creek (804-738-6827), and Americamps Lake Gaston (804-636-2668).

Resource Manager, John H. Kerr Reservoir, Route 1, Box 76, Boydton, VA 23917 (804-738-6143).

Lake Gaston Chamber of Commerce, P.O. Box 70, Littleton, NC 27850 (919-586-5711).

JAMES RIVER PARK

In the heart of Virginia's old Capital of the Confederacy, under the hum and whine of expressway traffic and in full view of the city skyline, the wild rapids of the James River pour over the Fall Line. The river then spreads out and transforms itself into the placid but mighty tidal James, capable of floating oceangoing ships into Hampton Roads, Chesapeake Bay, and eventually the Atlantic Ocean.

Bordering this historic and lively stretch of whitewater in downtown Richmond—a section cautiously explored by Capt. John Smith and the first English settlers—is a patchwork of green riverbanks and islands that form the sectionalized James River Park. A quiet refuge from city life, the park is stitched for five miles with birdsong, footbridges, giant boulders, and gurgling, winding waterways.

The park is accessible from ten points on both sides of the river. It's a refreshing mecca in summer heat for waders, sunbathers, tubers, snorkelers, kayakers, and bass anglers. (Some of the best smallmouth bass fishing in Virginia is found in this park. Several smallmouth of five pounds or more come from this stretch of the river each season.)

Little utilized are the opportunities to enjoy the natural world along the city's river property, where there's an abundance of wildlife, including otters, beavers, great blue herons, osprey, Canada geese, a variety of ducks, kingfishers, and an occasional bald eagle.

The park even boasts its own naturalist, Ralph White, winner of the Governor's Environmental Excellence Award.

Look him up—you'll find him intelligent and engaging, with a gentle nature that puts him in his element on a sunlit path beneath a canopy of river birch and sycamore.

For a peaceful natural experience even at peak visitor season, try the riverside trail from the Twenty-Second Street parking area near Lee Bridge on Riverside Drive. From the east end of the parking lot, follow the path across the footbridge and 200 yards upriver. If time allows, put a picnic lunch in your knapsack, detour out into the river on the concrete levee, and follow the trail upriver on the Goat Islands. Maps and trail guides are helpful for new visitors.

Bicycling is popular on scenic Belle Isle. Park your car on Tredegar Street on the north bank of the river and cross to the island.

Motorboats may be launched at Ancarrows Landing on the east end of Maury Street. Tubing and canoeing are good from Pony Pasture to Reedy Creek (see park map).

Because this is a city park, valuables should be locked out of sight in your car or trunk. Park officials ask that you not carry anything in glass containers and suggest that you wear wading shoes. Sunrise and sunset can be spectacular on the river. Bring a camera.

In late August and early September, this park is a paradise for pawpaw hunters. Though hard to find in many sections of Virginia today, the custardlike, sweet, edible fruit of this small tree is abundant here.

Where: Both sides of James River in Richmond. Parking for visitors center at Riverside Drive and Hillcrest Road, on south bank. Walk across railroad tracks and short distance east to visitors center.

Hours: Dawn until one hour after sunset, year-round. Generally speaking, visitors center Tuesday to Saturday year-round (call ahead for hours).

A mallard drake

Admission: Free.

Best time to visit: Spring and fall for hiking and wildlife observation, spring for whitewater boating, June and July for canoeing, July and August for snorkeling and tubing, fall for bicycling. June and July for smallmouth bass fishing. April and May for striped bass fishing. Saturdays, spring through fall, for programs.

Activities: Hiking, wildlife observation, wading, tubing, canoeing, snorkeling (brochure available), whitewater boating, motorboating in tidal water, fishing. Saturday interpretive programs spring through fall. Call for flyers, maps.

Concessions: Whitewater raft trips (804-222-7238), ropes challenge course (804-358-0577).

Pets: Leash must be in owner's possession. Okay to let controllable pet off leash.

For more information:

Ralph White, James River Park, City of Richmond, 700 Blanton Avenue, Richmond, VA 23221 (804-780-5311).

LAKE ANNA STATE PARK

When people in the gently rolling hill country of central Virginia think big boats, big water, and big fish, two words come to mind: Lake Anna.

Lake Anna is a 10,000-acre glittering jewel set in the green, undulating terrain of Louisa and Spotsylvania Counties. It is one of Virginia's most popular lakes for skiing and other water sports. Fishing for largemouth bass, crappie, and striped bass is big business on the lake. Several modern marinas with rental boats, motors, licenses, and bait shops cater to anglers.

Resident flocks of Canada geese spend the year at Lake Anna. The big birds with the distinctive white chin straps add a touch of wildness to the many coves of this sprawling lake. In spring, the gobble of wild turkeys drifts across the water, and

A wild turkey

deer sometimes come down to the lake's edge to drink late in the day.

On the north side of the lake off County 601 is Lake Anna State Park. The state park can accommodate only day-trippers, since there are no overnight facilities. Private campgrounds around the lake serve campers. The state park, however, is large and has ample room to develop its 2,058 acres and eight miles of shoreline.

Check out the wildlife and old mining exhibits at the visitors center, or stroll along an abandoned logging road that skirts the lake on one of the park's eight walking trails. Look for beaver cuttings along the water's edge. Beavers gnaw the bark around the base of trees, and can topple small trees, leaving stumps with characterstic cone-shaped tops.

If you aren't planning to use a boat and motor on Lake Anna, keep in mind the swimming beach, hiking trails, and lakeside picnic areas of the park.

Where: Central Virginia on north side of Lake Anna in Spotsylvania County off Route 601.

Hours: 8:00 A.M. until dusk daily, year-round.

Admission: Small parking fee. Fees for swimming and boat launching.

Best time to visit: Spring, summer, fall for lake activities. Anytime for hiking, fishing.

Activities: Nature exhibits, swimming beach, boat-launching ramp, lakeside picnic areas, hiking, panning for gold, environmental education pavilion available for groups.

Concessions: Concession and bathhouse complex.

Pets: Must be on leash. Prohibited in beach area.

Other: Lake Anna Family Campground (703-894-5529), pets permitted. Christopher Run Campground (703-894-4744), no pets. Several motels and marinas with boat rentals, bait, lures, fishing licenses on lake.

For more information:
Lake Anna State Park, 6800 Lawyers Road, Spotsylvania, VA 22553 (703-854-5503 or 804-786-1712).

LAKE PARKS OF CENTRAL PIEDMONT

Radiating out from the town of Farmville in central Virginia are three state parks—Twin Lakes, Bear Creek Lake, and Holliday Lake, each focused on water activity and each adjoining a state forest. In a 1993 *Virginia Wildlife* magazine article, fishing lakes at all three parks were included in a list of the state park system's best fishing holes.

Other popular activities at all of them include boating (electric motors only), lake swimming (lifeguarded beaches), camping, and hiking the gently rolling pine and hardwood forests characteristic of Virginia's Piedmont section.

Twin Lakes State Park

About seventeen miles southeast of Farmville, Twin Lakes State Park consists of Goodwin Lake and Prince Edward Lake. The swimming beach at twelve-acre Goodwin Lake has long been a big draw.

Isolated Prince Edward Lake, on the other hand, is designed primarily for fishing. It has a launch area for boats that can be carried in on a car top.

The 425-acre Twin Lakes State Park was founded in 1939 as two separate parks when land was purchased from struggling farmers during the Great Depression. In later years the parks were combined, resulting in one park with double facilities.

Improvements being made at Twin Lakes include installation of water and electric hookups for campgrounds and renovation of the Cedar Crest Conference Center. The center, which is available for rent, provides a private lake with six lakefront cabins.

Bear Creek Lake State Park

About twenty miles north of Farmville and less than an hour west of Richmond, Bear Creek Lake State Park is one of Virginia's best kept fishing secrets. Situated on a forty-acre lake, it has many of the offerings of the larger parks, but the masses have not yet discovered it. Fishing for largemouth bass, crappie, bream, and channel catfish is excellent. The park provides access to the Willis River Trail and other trails in the surrounding Cumberland State Forest, a popular hunting ground. Development of a hunter's campground is in the works.

Holliday Lake State Park

Northwest of Farmville and northeast of Appomattox is Holliday Lake State Park. Picturesque 150-acre Holliday Lake is deep and cold and has plenty of cover for fish. It is the second-cleanest lake in Virginia, according to chief ranger Paul Billings. (Mountain Lake in southwestern Virginia is number one.) "This lake is a real hidden treasure, and is underfished," said Billings.

The state game department stocks Holliday Lake annually with northern pike and channel catfish. Crappie grow big here too, and the lake holds largemouth bass and bream. A launch for car-top boats enables those who bring small boats to use the lake.

A weekend program of summer night fishing is popular. In July and August, the park stays open until midnight to allow anglers to fish while getting a break from the heat. For fishing information, contact Fish Division, Department of Game and

Inland Fisheries, P.O. Box 11104, Richmond, VA 23230-1104 (804-367-1000).

You might also want to take the Lake Trail to the north end of the lake. There you'll see signs of fresh beaver cuttings at the water's edge, and possibly even the animal's distinctive paw print. Look for the telltale webbing between the toes of the hind foot in the track. As you approach, don't be startled by a sudden, resounding Crack! as the beaver slaps the water with his flat tail. That's his alarm sound.

Northwest of Farmville is Amelia Wildlife Management Area, one of many such areas managed by the Virginia Department of Game and Inland Fisheries for hunting in fall as well as fishing and wildlife observation year-round. The property also has a public shooting range for sighting-in firearms, and boasts a challenging sporting clays course. Range reservations are required. The course is open Friday, Saturday, and Sunday. Call 804-367-8464 for prices and reservations.

Just minutes away from Holliday Lake State Park is famous Appomattox National Historical Park, located two miles east of Appomattox on State 24. Still standing is the house where the Civil War ended when Gen. Robert E. Lee surrendered to Gen. Ulysses S. Grant.

Where: Twin Lakes, from US 360 west of Burkeville in Prince Edward County, take County 613 north and County 629 east to the park. Bear Creek, from US 60 west of Richmond, go northwest on County 622, then southwest on County 629. Holliday Lake, go ten miles east of Appomattox on State 24, then turn right on County 626, left on County 640, and right on County 692.
Hours: 8:00 A.M. until dark for day use. Visitors center and overnight camping during summer season (opening and closing dates vary).
Admission: Small parking fee. Fee for camping, swimming.

Best time to visit: Warm weather for lake activities, anytime for trail use.

Activities: Freshwater fishing, lake swimming and boating (no gasoline motors), hiking, self-guiding trails, bicycling (Twin Lakes only), picnicking, camping, group camping and housekeeping cabins at Twin Lakes, interpretive programs, visitors center, environmental education, wheelchair access.

Concessions: Bike, canoe, rowboat, and paddleboat rental during summer (except no canoes at Twin Lakes), seasonal snack bar.

Pets: Must be on leash.

For more information:

Twin Lakes State Park, Route 2, Box 70, Green Bay, VA 23942 (804-392-3435 or 804-786-1712).

Bear Creek Lake State Park, Route 1, Box 253, Cumberland, VA 23040 (804-492-4410 or 804-786-1712).

Holliday Lake State Park, Route 2, Box 622, Appomattox, VA 24522 (804-248-6308 or 804-786-1712).

LEWIS GINTER BOTANICAL GARDEN

From an old estate on the north side of Virginia's capital city has come the lovely Lewis Ginter Botanical Garden. Owned briefly by Patrick Henry when he was governor, the garden was donated to the city of Richmond by its last owner, Miss Grace E. Arents, and named for her civic-minded uncle.

During the years between Miss Arents's death in 1926 and establishment of the garden in 1982, many of the original plantings were lost, but enough of the old trees and garden design remain to give this bright new development a historic flavor.

Pick up a brochure for the self-guided tour at the entrance and follow the undulating brick walkways, luring you first through the Henry M. Flagler Perennial Garden (nicknamed the "garden of gentle surprises"), beautiful even in midwinter with an impressive variety of evergreens.

Interested in wetlands and bogs? Take the boardwalk detour over the lake into the Martha and Reed West Island Garden, hop-scotching little islands of reeds and rushes, pitcher plants, and even Venus's flytraps. Then have a leisurely lunch in the Japanese-style Lora and Claiborne Robins Tea House overlooking the garden lake.

Depending on the season, you might wander down pathways of tulips and pansies, azaleas and rhododendrons, ferns and roses, daffodils or prize-winning daylilies. See more than 190 ivies in the Standard Reference Ivy Collection, accepted by the American Ivy Society as the standard by which all other collections are judged.

Enter the Bloemendaal House, a restored Victorian country home, furnished with period furniture.

Not only is the eighty-acre garden a botanical feast, but education and research are also prime objectives of the Lewis Ginter Botanical Society, Inc., the private foundation entrusted with the garden's care. For children and adults, the garden hosts education programs, dances, art, music, and other special events.

We recommend Lewis Ginter as a must-see for those who love flowers, plants, and landscaping. Everything is first-rate, the quest for perfection obvious.

Where: North Richmond, on Lakeside Avenue, just north of intersection with Hilliard Road.
Hours: 9:30 A.M. to 4:30 P.M. Monday to Saturday, 1:00 P.M. to 4:30 P.M. Sunday. Closed Christmas (usually for two days) and New Year's Day. Teahouse closed in January. Bloemendaal House closed during special events.
Admission: Small fee.
Best time to visit: All seasons. Flowers bloom even in winter.
Activities: Touring garden's floral display and turn-of-the-century

country estate, children's garden, visitors center, horticulture classes, special events.

Concessions: Teahouse lunch, gift shop.

Pets: Not allowed.

Other: Nearby Bryan Park Azalea Garden, in spring.

For more information:

Lewis Ginter Botanical Garden, 1800 Lakeside Avenue, Richmond, VA 23228 (804-262-9887).

MAYMONT

What do black bears, politicians, and formal gardens have in common?

All provide entertainment in downtown Richmond.

When the Virginia General Assembly is in session each January and February, politicians in their finest plumage may be observed at the state capitol.

Fifteen minutes away is Maymont, with its nineteenth-century Dooley mansion, formal Japanese and Italian gardens, nature center, animal exhibits, and arboretum. Maymont is 100 acres of delight and balm to the senses, sandwiched between the railroad and freeways in the heart of Richmond.

To properly enjoy it all, you really need an entire day. But any part of Maymont could provide a pleasant morning, afternoon, or even a restful lunch break.

Exit I-64 or I-95 if you're on a journey to somewhere else. Stroll through the thirty-three opulent, well-appointed rooms of the Victorian Romanesque mansion willed to the city intact when its owner died. Visit the carriage house, made from stone quarried on the estate, and see a working collection of antique carriages. Pack a picnic lunch and wander down columned breezeways in the formal gardens. Pause on the steps beside a tumbling waterfall, or sit beside pools of lily pads while munching a sandwich.

From over the hill at Maymont may come the sound of a bugling elk. Follow that wild call to the outdoor habitats, where you can see wildlife native to Virginia. There are black bears, foxes, beavers, bobcats, hawks, owls, and an aviary that you can enter to be close to ducks and birds. Unlike many zoo animals, the Maymont animals were orphaned or rescued, and for various reasons could not be released back into the wild. White-tailed deer, elk, and bison have whole hillsides and woods to roam. Bears have huge boulders and a large pool from the estate's old stone quarry, similar to their native habitat. Wild deer from surrounding woods have been known to jump the fence to join the Maymont herd.

If you have children who want to touch everything they see, leave time for the children's farm, where they can pet sheep and have their faces licked by goats.

There's an indoor nature center with a large fish tank and other exhibits, and friendly staff to tell you about the wild animals you've seen.

Come to see the Maymont Flower and Garden Show, listed in the *New York Times* as one of the country's top twelve such shows. Hosted by the Maymont Foundation, it is held annually in mid-February at The Richmond Centre, 400 East Marshall Street in Richmond.

Where: Two miles west of downtown Richmond. From I-64 and I-95, take exit 78 and follow the Boulevard south two miles to Columbus statue. Follow Maymont signs through Byrd Park and into parking area at Hampton Street gate.

Hours: 10:00 A.M. to 5:00 P.M. daily November 1 to March 31, 10:00 A.M. to 7:00 P.M. daily April 1 to October 31. Indoor exhibits and museum store closed Mondays.

Admission: Free (donations encouraged). Small fee for carriage rides and tram tours. Fee for group tours.

Best time to visit: Spring for formal gardens, early December for Christmas open house. For wildlife observation, come early on hot days.

Activities: Walking tour of nineteenth-century mansion and estate, including Japanese and Italian gardens. Carriage rides, nature center, museum store, arboretum, animal exhibits, children's farm.

Concessions: The Emporium (museum store). Spring to fall, outdoor Carriage Court Cafe.

Pets: Not allowed.

For more information:

Maymont Foundation, 1700 Hampton Street, Richmond, VA 23220 (804-358-7166).

POCAHONTAS STATE PARK

Beware when someone in downtown Richmond says, "Let's do lunch," then shakes a bag of the city's famous Bill's Barbeque sandwiches under your nose.

He or she just might be taking you, not to the woodshed, but to the woods.

Pocahontas State Park is that close. Nowhere else in the state could you sneak away from a boring legislative hearing in the Virginia General Assembly, whip out to a state park less than thirty minutes from the noise and pace of the big city, and brownbag it under a leafy canopy while deer, squirrels, even an osprey or two watch from the shores of a beautiful lake.

(Just so neighboring localities won't feel slighted, it ought to be said that Pocahontas State Park is equally close to Petersburg, Hopewell, and Colonial Heights, all just south of Richmond.)

Because Pocahontas serves such a sprawling metropolitan area, it is one of Virginia's busiest parks. In fact, the park has practically been loved to death since the Civilian Conservation

Corps built the recreation area in the 1930s. When the park opened in 1941, more than a quarter million people poured in the first year.

But by following our general rule of visiting anyplace near a metropolitan area in the off-season, we practically had the 7,600 acres of this largest of state parks to ourselves on a pleasant late-fall day. A father and son were strapping on their helmets to try out the three-mile Old Mill Bicycle Trail winding through the woods around twenty-four-acre Beaver Lake. The park's relatively flat trails are also perfect for cross-country skiing.

The Awareness Walk, a paved trail from the visitors center parking lot down to the amphitheater and on to the Beaver Lake spillway, is wheelchair-accessible, though a bit steep. This path ties in to the Spillway Nature Trail, which skirts one edge of the lake and passes by a small pier. There, you can while away an afternoon with a favorite book while a breeze faintly stirs the tops of loblolly pine, American holly, and beech trees, or ponder such weighty matters as where the residents of the lake's wood-duck boxes go in the winter.

The park also has the very popular, serpentine, 150-acre Swift Creek Lake. In summer, canoes, rowboats, and paddle-boats are available for rent, or you may bring your own. Fishing is making a comeback from the draining and restocking that took place in early 1993. A child in a baby stroller and his young mother were the only two people near the lake this day. With its two playgrounds, huge swimming complex, and children's nature programs, the park does seem the perfect place to bring children.

Pocahontas is undergoing a much-needed facelift and renovation. The park is getting a new lease on life as more than $9 million in state bond money is being spent for new campgrounds, underground electric lines, trails, a playground, and maybe even a staging area for a privately developed equestrian center. Additionally, the park is getting a new environmental education

A handsome, raucous bluejay

center, a renovated nature center and amphitheater, a group camp and cabin area with dining hall and bathhouse.

Walk the trails respectfully – there are ghosts about. Like many rivers, lakes, and parks in central and Tidewater Virginia, this place was named for a Native American whose people lived on the land centuries before the first English settlers arrived at nearby Jamestown in 1607.

Legend has it that Pocahontas, daughter of powerful Chief

Powhatan, fell in love with and saved Capt. John Smith's life. Whether or not she intervened between her father and Smith may never be known, but this is fact: Pocahontas married John Rolphe and became one of the first Native Americans to return to London with the early settlers. She died in England, of smallpox, in 1617. The son of Pocahontas, educated in England, returned to Virginia and became an important player in the early affairs of the state.

Where: Chesterfield County, about twenty miles south of Richmond. Take exit 6 off I-95, go west on State 10, then west on County 655 (Beach Road) to park entrance.

Hours: 8:00 A.M. until dark daily, year-round. Visitors center, swimming, boat rental, interpretive programs, Memorial Day weekend to Labor Day. Camping seasonal; contact park for dates.

Admission: Small parking fee. Camping and pool fee.

Best time to visit: Anytime for hiking, fishing. Spring through fall for camping. Memorial Day to Labor Day for visitors center, swimming, interpretive programs.

Activities: Largest swimming complex in Virginia, public or private (17,500 square feet of swimming area.) Picnic shelters, shaded campsites, fishing, hiking, bicycle and cross-country ski trails, wheelchair-access trail. Interpretive programs including guided nature hikes, slide presentations, night hikes, canoe and paddleboat tours, campfire and children's programs, environmental education. Rental cabins available for groups of 20 to 120, overnight or daily basis. Ecology camp for groups by prior arrangement. Hunting allowed outside recreation area of park.

Concessions: Concession building operates seasonally. Seasonal rental of bicycles, canoes, paddleboats, rowboats.

Pets: Must be on leash.

Other: Nearby Swift Creek Lake Wildlife Management Area; Chesterfield County Museum, (antique toys, woodcarvings, and

Victorian clothing); Magnolia Grange, a plantation house built in 1822 and a National Historic Landmark.

For more information:

Pocahontas State Park, 10300 Park Road, Chesterfield, VA 23832 (804-796-4255 or 804-786-1712).

3

Tidewater Region

BACK BAY NATIONAL WILDLIFE REFUGE
AND FALSE CAPE STATE PARK

This remote stretch of Atlantic seacoast, which includes Back
Bay National Wildlife Refuge and adjoining False Cape State
Park, represents two separate entities on maps and in the minds
of state and federal bureaucrats.

The refuge and park, however, are one and the same to the
wild species that live here. The wildlife area is part of the sandy
string of barrier islands that protects mainland Virginia and other
East Coast states from the ceaseless smashing of the Atlantic
Ocean surf. The refuge is about 8,000 acres and the state park is
an additional 4,321 acres. Refuge and park lie end to end, with
nothing but trail signs to remind you that you're leaving one and
entering the other.

With habitats including beach, dunes, woodland, and
marsh, this is an especially good area for a diverse wildlife population, including osprey, deer, wild ponies, feral pigs, cottonmouth moccasins, snow geese, Canada geese, tundra swans,

many seagulls and ducks, songbirds, and even endangered species such as loggerhead sea turtles, piping plovers, peregrine falcons, and bald eagles. Bring binoculars.

Back Bay

Most people enter Back Bay by car, drive to the visitors contact station to park, then walk the salt marsh and woodland trails. But don't drive too quickly past another excellent place to see wildlife—the entrance road. Better yet, bring your bicycles (we rent them in nearby Sandbridge) and pedal this paved road leisurely to the parking lot.

Then you can stop along the way and identify that towhee in the dune thickets, shrilly pronouncing its own name. You can find the catbird, making its telltale mewling sound. Maybe you'll even spot a yellow-breasted chat atop a tall tree, proclaiming its territory with a variety of squawks and chirps. The chat's call suggests a mockingbird that has a repertoire of unusual night sounds.

Also, in the canal alongside the road you can find the busy muskrat, turtles sunning on logs, wading birds such as the comical little green heron and the elegant great blue heron, as well as the great egret, stark white against the dark growth behind it. Most of the white-tailed deer we've seen in Back Bay have been within sight of this road. Rabbits are everywhere; they scarcely give bicyclists a second glance.

In spring and summer, the air near the parking lot is full of darting purple martins that nest in the apartment birdhouses around the visitors center.

When you arrive at the parking area, look out over Back Bay for big osprey nests atop posts in the distance. You may see the large dark bird, mostly white underneath, hovering about 100 feet above the surface, then plunging into the water after a fish.

Many such dives are unproductive, but when the osprey is successful, it struggles to gain altitude with its catch, turning the head of the fish forward in its talons to reduce air resistance.

False Cape

Isolated False Cape State Park, with its wild dunes, its forest of loblolly pines, maples, and live oak trees, is closed to motorized traffic. The only way to enter the park is by boat or by walking or bicycling about four miles through the refuge on sand and gravel trails.

Several paths thread this fine example of unspoiled Atlantic coast. You'll walk along sand dunes, barrier beaches, woodland, and salt marsh (75 percent of the refuge is marsh). An elevated boardwalk leads across the marshland to the Atlantic surf, where sandpipers forage in the surf and brown pelicans and osprey do Olympic-class dives for fish. Some days, schools of porpoise roll and turn just offshore.

Besides walking or biking the park and refuge, another way to see the area is by water. When the wind is light, canoes and kayaks are perfect craft to explore the miles of coves and scores of small islands in shallow Back Bay on the west side. The bay is rich in nutrients—a nursery and feeding ground for mammals, fish, wading birds, and many other animals.

To access False Cape by boat across Back Bay, use the park boat docks at Barbour Hill, False Cape Landing, and Wash Woods. Several boat ramps are available off Princess Anne Road on the west side of the bay outside of the refuge and park. (Overnight parking is not allowed at Back Bay.)

Bikes are available for rent in nearby Sandbridge, and canoes and kayaks are available in Virginia Beach.

No concessions are available inside the refuge and park. Primitive camping is allowed in the state park, but you have to-.

COTTONMOUTH MOCCASIN

We saw our first cottonmouth moccasin in Back Bay refuge. You can spend a lifetime in Virginia's outdoors, and unless you come to this southeastern corner, you'll see only two poisonous snakes—the rattler and the copperhead. The cottonmouth makes up for its absence elsewhere in the state with its abundance in the Back Bay area. This one was in a marsh pond encircled by a hiking trail. So buoyant is the cottonmouth that it seemed to float on top of the water. The snake appeared unperturbed by our presence. In fact, it headed in our direction, then came to the edge of the pond and disappeared in the reeds. We suddenly remembered another trail we wanted to hike.

But don't let the snakes keep you away. This is truly wild country, changed little since the day in 1607 when Capt. John Smith and his tiny ships came slowly up the Virginia coast, looking for a place to anchor.

---

come in by water or hike/bike just over four miles from the refuge entrance, plus carry everything you'll need, including water. One gallon of water per person per day is recommended. You will also need to obtain a camping permit in person from Seashore State Park in Virginia Beach. In addition, ask for the Barbour Hill Nature Trail booklet, which will make the changing habitat along the way more understandable. Bring insect repellent. In warm weather, mosquitoes and biting flies can be a nuisance. Sunscreen and a hat are also a good idea in summer.

Where: Extreme southeastern corner of state, south of Virginia Beach. At Sandbridge, follow Sandpiper Road about four miles south to refuge. False Cape accessible by hiking, biking, or boating south of Back Bay refuge.

Hours: Dawn to dusk daily. Back Bay visitor contact station

8:00 A.M. to 4:00 P.M. weekdays, 9:00 A.M. to 4:00 P.M. weekends (closed Saturdays December to March, closed holidays except Memorial Day, July 4, and Labor Day). False Cape and Back Bay refuge are closed in early October for controlled deer hunt.

Admission: On foot or bicycle, $2.00 per family; $4.00 per car; under 16, free. Camping fee for park.

Best time to visit: Anytime for wildlife observation, hiking, bicycle trails. Spring for ducks with young, nesting osprey, peak of songbird and shorebird migration, blooming of rare orchids. Summer for nesting sea turtles, wading birds, songbirds. Fall and winter for snow geese, Canada geese, tundra swans, northern harriers, and rafts of ducks.

Activities: Refuge has foot trails with two boardwalks leading to beach, visitor contact center, surf and freshwater fishing, small boating in bay (no trailers, no ramp), bicycling (some trails closed seasonally to protect wildlife), slide talks, films, outdoor classroom activities for groups by reservation. State park is accessible by foot, bicycle, or boat; primitive camping including beachfront camping by permit only, self-guided hiking trails, bicycle trails, freshwater and saltwater fishing, interpretive seasonal programs, environmental education center, pontoon boat available for on-water educational activities.

Concessions: Bike and boat rental available in Sandbridge and Virginia Beach.

Pets: Prohibited April 1 to September 30 and permitted October 1 to March 31 on leash.

Other: Canoeing on nearby North Landing River, a designated state scenic river.

For more information:

Refuge Manager, Back Bay National Wildlife Refuge, P.O. Box 6286, Virginia Beach, VA 23456-0286 (804-721-2412).

False Cape State Park, 4001 Sandpiper Road, Virginia

Beach, VA 23456 (804-726-7128). For camping permits and information, contact Seashore State Park, 2500 Shore Drive, Virginia Beach, VA 23451 (804-481-2131).

North Landing River Natural Area Preserve, Department of Conservation and Recreation, Natural Heritage Division, 1500 East Main Street, Suite 312, Richmond, VA 23219 (804-786-7951).

CALEDON NATURAL AREA

Our lasting impression of Caledon Natural Area is awe. Not breath-grabbing, Grand Canyon awe. No, it's more subtle than that.

The feeling of reverence was inspired by the huge trees clustered in sections of forested slopes dipping down to the Potomac River. Trees that at times attract eagles.

Months after our visit, Caledon drifts through the mind like primordial half memories. Some of the natural area is virgin forest, untouched by ax or saw for more than 100 years. There are massive hardwoods, and tulip poplars as straight and tall as the Pillars of Hercules.

The eastern United States, Virginia included, has been logged, burned, and cut over several times since the first settlers landed almost 400 years ago. At Caledon, almost every tree in the state is represented, and many of the trees here heard the rattle of Civil War muskets.

There's a cathedral-like ambiance. Without thinking, you lower your voice a couple of decibels. A shout here would be as gauche and out of place as a rebel yell in the Taj Mahal.

But the natural area's biggest attraction is the bald eagles. In summer, the river bluffs of Caledon and the surrounding area are home to one of the largest concentrations of eagles on the East

Coast. When summer brings migratory fish surging up the broad Potomac River, as many as sixty eagles spend the season perched on the cliffs or in the riverside trees.

Park personnel go to great pains to see that the bird that is our national symbol is not disturbed. You're not permitted to just wander around by the river where the eagles are fishing while your brother-in-law—the one who learned to whisper in a sawmill—tries to interest you in a Florida time-share.

Guided eagle tours provide public access without alarming the birds. They're available from mid-June through September and take about one-and-a-half hours. There's a fee, and reservations are recommended. Binoculars and spotting scopes are

---

EYEBALLING EAGLES
Bald eagles aren't bald.

It's mildly comforting to know that these fierce-looking birds with the seven-foot wingspreads aren't riding the air currents looking for instant hair-in-a-can as advertised on TV.

The word *bald* refers to the eagle's white head. Bald is an old Middle English word meaning white. Young birds don't develop the distinctive white head and neck until maturity, or about their fourth year.

Because Virginia has a growing, though modest, bald eagle population, chances of seeing one of the magnificent birds are improving. Chesapeake Bay and the tidal rivers that feed the bay are prime eagle territory. Virginia officials estimate there are 300 pairs of breeding eagles in the Chesapeake Bay region, evenly split between the Virginia and the Maryland sides.

If you want to go in search of eagles, keep in mind that they follow the great schools of migratory fish that enter the Chesapeake and its feeder rivers. Late April to mid-October are optimum times, though a few birds hang around all year. Likely places to see them are on the James River below Richmond, in the Caledon Natural Area of the Potomac River, and along the tidal Rappahannock River.

available. Allow a whole day to see this natural area if you can, because there are five beautiful hiking trails through the climax forests.

Lesser known are the 120 other bird species that have been identified in the 2,579-acre Caledon Natural Area, including such interesting characters as the yellow-breasted chat, the American redstart, the woodcock, and the Acadian flycatcher. Ask at the visitors center for a bird checklist.

Whereas many state and national parks are designed to entertain with swimming pools and beaches, Caledon is different. Caledon is designed to make you think.

Where: From I-95 at Fredericksburg, take State 3 east, State 206 north, and State 218 east to the park.

Hours: Hiking trails and picnic area 8:00 A.M. until dusk year-round; visitors center Memorial Day to Labor Day; eagle tours 10:00 A.M. and 2:00 P.M., Thursday to Sunday, mid-June to Labor Day, reservations encouraged.

Admission: Modest fee for eagle tour, children under six free when accompanied by adult.

Best time to visit: Mid-June to September for eagle tours.

Activities: Eagle and bird observation, day and night hiking, picnicking, interpretive programs including night hikes, bonfire programs, and stargazing, visitors center exhibits, environmental education facilities, school programs by prior arrangement.

Concessions: Vending machines.

Pets: Must be on leash.

Other: Visitors center in turn-of-the-century Smoot House, with decor of the era; wildlife art exhibition each December.

For more information:

Caledon Natural Area, 11617 Caledon Road, King George, VA 22485 (703-663-3861 or 804-786-1712).

CHESAPEAKE BAY

The mighty Chesapeake. Subject of poem, story, and song, Chesapeake Bay represents a fascinating, almost foreign, country for those Virginians, and others, whose ancestors did not go down to the sea in ships.

Visitors from inland may be forgiven for thinking they're looking out on a world wondrously different and strange when they stand on the spray-flecked Chesapeake Bay Bridge-Tunnel and watch a nuclear submarine from the Norfolk fleet go by half submerged while gulls cry and great ocean-dwelling fish— channel bass and cobia—swim underneath.

The Chesapeake is too vast, too diverse to be described in a single chapter. A book is needed. No, several books. The best we can do is point you in the direction of a few of our favorite places on the bay. This is, after all, the largest estuary in North America—180 miles long and 30 miles wide in places. The Chesapeake is bordered by 8,000 miles of shoreline. That's more than twice the distance across America.

More than fifty rivers and hundreds of small creeks feed the bay. Half a million acres of tidal wetlands line the shore. The bay drains 64,000 square miles of Virginia, Maryland, Pennsylvania, and West Virginia. More than 13 million people live in its watershed.

Incidentally, good books about the bay are available in the library and in bookstores. James Michener's *Chesapeake* is a fine overview of the bay's history in novel form. You might also want to check out Tom Horton's *Bay Country,* or William W. Warner's *Beautiful Swimmers.*

In addition to being a busy waterway for oceangoing commercial and military ships, the bay is the summer home for several species of endangered or threatened sea turtles. It's the

BEAUTIFUL SWIMMERS

It would take a writer with the soul of a poet to suggest that the Chesapeake Bay blue crab exemplifies beauty.

William W. Warner did just that in his Pulitzer prizewinning book, *Beautiful Swimmers*. The book remains the definitive study of one of the bay's most interesting and delicious sandwich-sized residents. The Chesapeake, says Warner, provides more crabs for human consumption than any other body of water in the world, great oceans included. An estimated 95 million pounds of these tasty crustaceans are harvested from the bay each year.

With its eyes on stalks, a mouth that works like a pair of scissors, and one outsized reaching and probing claw, a blue crab looks like something out of a bad Japanese horror movie. It is perpetually pugnacious and will enthusiastically pinch you as well as your dog.

A crab's habits aren't exactly what you'd call mainstream. It sleeps in the bottom mud all winter, migrates up the bay in warm weather from ocean to tidal rivers and back while reproducing and riding piggyback, and remakes itself several times during its lifetime by shedding its old skin and growing a new one.

From thousands of docks and fishing piers along Chesapeake Bay, delighted children pull blue crabs from the water, on chicken necks tied to string.

Yet these same crabs are extremely hard to catch commercially in significant numbers. Just ask any tough old waterman who has chosen the ancient art of crabbing to pay the bills and finance his children's education. He'll tell you that he has nothing but admiration for the blue crab's intelligence, unpredictability, and pure cussedness.

Sample some crab cakes while you're near the bay. Or try a softshell crab sandwich. Most bay restaurants serve crabmeat in one fashion or another.

Try catching your own. Any grocery store or sporting goods store in the area can provide the necessary string and bait. They'll also throw in elementary tips for successful crabbing. No license is needed.

winter resting place for more than half a million migratory waterfowl in the Atlantic Flyway, including as many as 10,000 tundra swans that arrive near Thanksgiving and return north about mid-March.

The bay is also a thriving nursery and feeding ground for more than 300 species of finfish and a tremendous variety of shellfish. Incidentally, those ubiquitous softball-sized floats you see scattered about the bay are color markers on watermen's crab pots.

Referring to the bay's abundant life — from giant choppers, or bluefish, and flounder to the famous blue crab and Chesapeake oyster — H. L. Mencken once described this estuary where freshwater and saltwater mix as nothing less than "an immense protein factory." The world dines on eels, oysters, blue crabs, and fish caught here. Striped bass taken from the surf of New England most likely began life in Chesapeake Bay, since this is where 90 percent of East Coast stripers are spawned.

If you're interested in anything from a moonlight cruise to a fishing trip, several hundred U.S. Coast Guard–approved charter boats operate throughout the bay.

One source of information is the Virginia Charter Boat Association, HCR Box 394-I, Deltaville, VA 23043 (804-776-9850).

Another is the Virginia Saltwater Fishing Tournament, 968 Oriole Drive, Suite 102, Virginia Beach, VA 23451 (804-491-5160).

Also ready to help is the Virginia Division of Tourism, Bell Tower, Capitol Grounds, P.O. Box 798, Richmond, VA 23219 (804-786-4484).

Ask what services are available on the bay when you stop at marinas, fishing piers, sporting goods stores, gas stations, and restaurants. Assume that Capt. John Smith was right when he wrote in 1608 that "heaven and earth never agreed better to frame a place for man's habitation" than the mighty Chesapeake. Furthermore, take the attitude that you don't want to miss any of it.

Chesapeake Bay Bridge–Tunnel

One of the more unusual places in Virginia to fish—or for that matter, to watch the nautical world go by—is the Sea Gull Pier, located practically in the middle of Chesapeake Bay.

The pier is a concrete-legged appendage that sticks out from the Chesapeake Bay Bridge–Tunnel, a fascinating aquatic highway that alternately skims the waves and burrows beneath the cold, salty water of the Chesapeake Bay.

The bridge-tunnel is one of the seven modern wonders of the world. More than seventeen miles long, it is one of the world's largest complexes of its kind. In addition to being a thrilling drive, traveling over and under the bay saves nearly 100 miles and two hours of driving between the megalopolis of Virginia Beach–Norfolk and points north of the Delaware Memorial Bridge.

Millions of tons of boulders were used to build four islands. The stone jetties of the islands became a banquet table for migrating fish. A free fishing pier was added on the main island, as well as a decent restaurant and a big gift shop catering to tourists.

One morning just after daybreak, we stood on the end of the fog-bound Sea Gull Pier and decided this was a darn good place to greet the day.

A couple of navy ships eased by, close enough (or so it seemed) for us to reach out and touch them with a fishing rod. An oceangoing tanker with what appeared to be Russian lettering also passed. So did an incredibly noisy military hovercraft, similar to the ones used to cross the English Channel. When an aircraft carrier materialized from the fog and slowly vanished, it seemed that a city had floated by.

WHALE-WATCHING

In Virginia the industry is just getting started. Since about 1990, large comfortable headboats (which charge by the passenger, or "head") have been transporting people offshore to watch migrating whales move slowly north.

Mostly, the whales are humpbacks. These whales—some as long a tractor trailer—follow schools of mackerel and herring, feeding as they go. The ocean near the mouth of Chesapeake Bay and off the resort coast of Virginia is usually brimming with small bait fish during the months of January and February, when whale-watching peaks.

It's cold on the Atlantic Ocean in winter, so dress warmly and wear water-repellent gear. The headboats have warm cabin quarters where you can grab something hot if it gets too raw on the deck outside.

For boat rates and schedules, contact Virginia Marine Science Museum, 717 General Booth Boulevard, Virginia Beach, VA 23451 (804-437-4949).

Not everything associated with the bridge-tunnel is man-made. On another visit we watched a humongous loggerhead turtle, just in from the sea and big as a dinner table, swim lethargically underneath the pier. Even whales and porpoise are spotted occasionally.

The only trouble with fishing or sight-seeing off the Sea Gull Pier on the bridge-tunnel is that, although use of the pier is free, it costs $10.00 per car to get on the bridge-tunnel and take US 13 across Chesapeake Bay. Of course, if you take along another angler—or a significant other who likes ships and sunrises and sea turtles—you can share the cost.

For a brochure and map, write to Chesapeake Bay Bridge–Tunnel, Cape Charles, VA 23310.

Tangier Island

If you've read literature on Chesapeake Bay and tried to imagine the venerable hunting and fishing villages of several generations ago, you must visit Tangier Island.

This is no Williamsburg "restored" with Rockefeller money. The lone town of Tangier on Tangier Island, with its 850 full-time residents, sits in the exact middle of Chesapeake Bay, making it in many ways one of the more remote areas in Virginia. Tangier looks, tastes, and smells like the wonderfully diverse bay itself.

Boat and plane are the only ways to reach the island. On the unpaved streets and roads, dirt bikes and electric golf carts serve instead of cars, because every gallon of gas, every spark plug, must be brought from the mainland.

Just a year after landing at Jamestown, Capt. John Smith was nosing around the Chesapeake when he discovered this mile-wide and three-and-a-half-mile-long island. He named it Tangier. The island had been used for centuries by the native Pocomoke for fishing and hunting. In 1686, just seventy-nine years after the arrival of Englishmen at Jamestown, a family named Crockett from Cornwall, England, came to Tangier to live.

The rich oyster and crab grounds surrounding Tangier attracted other families. The island has always been largely self-sufficient, and until the twentieth century, contact and commerce with mainland Virginia, and thus the world beyond the bay's horizon, was limited. Even today the people of Tangier speak with a lingering trace of Elizabethan English.

Tangier remains a romantic destination for thousands of tourists each summer. The town's small white houses, quaint narrow streets, two churches, lone school (kindergarten through high school), and rows of workboats tied to docks show that it is a genuine Chesapeake Bay fishing village whose very existence remains tied to the bay itself.

Walking tours are popular on Tangier, or a minibus will carry you around. A cruise boat, the *Chesapeake Breeze*, leaves the historic mainland fishing town of Reedville daily at 10:00 A.M. and returns at 3:45 P.M. The trip across the bay takes one and a half hours. A guide will meet you at the dock at Tangier and show you around for two and a half hours.

Do not take along peanut butter sandwiches. On the island is the modest white frame Chesapeake House restaurant, which serves its famous seafood dinners family-style. Over the past 200 years, Tangier residents have developed no talent for ruining delicate seafood. The meal will be one of the most memorable parts of the trip.

Before leaving the island, stand on the dock and look out toward mainland Virginia more than a dozen miles over the western horizon. Picture, if you can, winters when the bay freezes and contact with the larger world is cut off for days at a time.

What happens when someone gets acute appendicitis? Or a toothache? Or a baby is due? It's the sort of thing that'll keep you humble.

For reservations on the cruise boat, contact Tangier & Chesapeake Cruises, Warsaw, VA 22572 (804-333-4656). For Tangier information, contact Tangier Island, 2 Market Street, Tangier Island, VA 23440 (804-787-7911).

Bethel Beach Natural Area Preserve

On the western shore of Chesapeake Bay in Mathews County, peregrine falcons and bald eagles fly over salt marshes on the narrow peninsula that is Bethel Beach Natural Area Preserve. The waters of Winter Harbor to the west and south provide food for wintering loons, grebes, and sea ducks. In summer, the oystercatcher feeds on shellfish on the preserve's sandy beach, and the black skimmer soars low over the bay, deftly gleaning its prey from the surface with its lower mandible.

The natural area protects rare marsh birds and birds that nest in colonies, as well as a rare coastal insect, the northeastern beach tiger beetle, and a rare beach plant, seabeach knotweed.

The fifty-acre preserve is managed by the Virginia Department of Conservation and Recreation and is open year-round. Access to the lower portion of the property is prohibited from May through mid-September to help such species as the vulnerable least tern, which lays its eggs on the open sand. Dogs must be on a leash in this fragile environment.

The preserve is bordered on the north by County 609. For more information, contact the Department of Conservation and Recreation, Division of Natural Heritage, 1500 East Main Street, Suite 312, Richmond, VA 23219 (804-786-7951).

CHINCOTEAGUE NATIONAL WILDLIFE REFUGE

It's a little confusing, but Chincoteague National Wildlife Refuge (operated by the U.S. Fish and Wildlife Service) is actually part of Assateague Island, the barrier island just east of the town and the island of Chincoteague.

The refuge makes up the Virginia portion of Assateague. On the thin strip of land extending north into Maryland are two more public areas, Assateague Island National Seashore, managed by the National Park Service, and Assateague State Park, managed by the Maryland Department of Natural Resources.

The refuge, with its freshwater impoundments and wild salt marshes, is a haven for waterfowl and bird-watchers. Birds and animals are surprisingly tolerant of human intrusion here.

On an April visit, from just twenty feet away we watched pairs of Canada geese in the Piney Island marsh nibbling something in black ooze that only geese would find tasty. Later, while photographing running wild ponies kicking up spray along the marsh's edge, we had another close encounter. A great egret landed in the shallows, almost too close for our 500mm lens. The bird speared a fish with its rapier-like beak, tossed the prize in the air, and swallowed it headfirst. With its elegant, sleek form perfectly reflected in the slate-gray water, the giant bird remained for a long moment — seemingly oblivious to the whirring sound of the camera's motor drive — before lifting off with barely audible strokes of great wings. A photographer's dream.

An egret searching for lunch

Last fall, we were stunned again at the ease of approaching great blue herons wading in the canals along the hiking trails, various ducks diving in shallow lagoons, and roosting egrets adorning bare branches like oversized cotton balls.

Attracting attention on the lawn in front of the refuge headquarters were tiny Sika. The Sika resemble deer but are actually Oriental elk released on the island in 1923; they now inhabit the pine forests here. When someone gets a little too close, they spring away on all fours as if on pogo sticks, but they come right back as soon as the intruder retreats.

The wild ponies are equally approachable. In fact, the rangers beg visitors to keep their distance to avoid the chance of being bitten or kicked, and to protect the animals themselves, which occasionally are killed by cars while panhandling.

WILD PONIES OF ASSATEAGUE

It was here at Assateague that Misty of book and movie fame lived.

The real origin of these wild ponies is a mystery. They appear to come from domesticated stock that Eastern Shore farmers put on the island to graze as early as the seventeenth century. In this way, early settlers could avoid building fences and paying the mainland taxes.

According to legend, a Spanish galleon with a cargo of mustangs wrecked off the island coast in the sixteenth century. At any rate, the hardy ponies have been wild for generations and are well adapted to the extremes of barrier island weather, subsisting on a diet of marsh and dune grasses.

There are two herds on Assateague—one in Maryland and one in Virginia, separated by fencing. The Virginia herd is rounded up each July and forced to swim the channel to Chincoteague Island, where the new foals are sold at auction. Profits go to the Chincoteague Volunteer Fire Company, which owns the herd. Controlling the herd size this way prevents the horses from damaging the island ecosystem.

A short walking trail leads to the red-and-white-striped Assateague Light, where art exhibits are held on some summer and fall weekends. Another interesting path is the three-mile "wildlife loop," which winds around Snow Goose Pool. Walkers and bicyclists have the place to themselves until 3:00 P.M. each day, when vehicles are allowed in.

The refuge has two visitors centers—one near the entrance (open daily 9:00 A.M. to 4:00 P.M.) and another at the far end, at Tom's Cove (open daily 9:00 A.M. to 5:00 P.M.). Over the dunes to the east is the Atlantic Ocean and some of the most pristine beaches on the East Coast.

If you enjoy beach walking, you have thirty-seven miles of it on Assateague Island. With a permit, you can backpack right up into Maryland to a campsite. Overnight camping is not permitted on the Virginia end of the island.

When you ask for a permit at Tom's Cove Visitor Center, be sure to obtain information and maps, because it's a long hike (thirteen miles to the first site), and setting up camp in sand is unique. Seashore camping can provide pleasant memories for years—or be a vacation to forget. Come prepared to provide your own water and shade, to repel biting insects (which can be a problem from mid-May to October), and to secure your tent with long wooden sand stakes. The stakes can be purchased at outfitters and hardware stores. We can say from experience that you don't want to be caught in a windstorm with nothing but puny little tent stakes keeping nylon between you and the elements.

Three oceanside and four bayside campgrounds may be accessed by backpackers (or canoeists on the bay side) from May 31 to October 31.

If you've never been crabbing or clamming, you might be surprised at just how much fun it is to gather your own seafood dinner from the shallow coves of the refuge. Find out from the ranger at Tom's Cove Visitor Center which areas are best. Simplicity is part of the appeal. Equipment requirements are minimal: for crabbing, a chicken neck on a line or string and a net with a handle; for clamming, a rake. Actually, you can feel around in the muck for clams with just your toes, but some folks prefer tools.

To collect crabs, just toss out the bait a few feet away, keep the line taut until you feel the crab, and very gently pull it to you. With your other hand (or with the help of a partner), bring the net slowly up under the crab. Don't forget a container for your catch.

The little town of Chincoteague is interesting in its own right. Although it caters more to tourists now than when we first visited in the sixties, it still retains much of the character of former days, when the tough and independent islanders made their living solely from the sea. There are some outstanding seafood restaurants here, commercial campgrounds, grocery stores, shops, boutiques, and other attractions. For brochures or suggestions, contact the Chincoteague Island Chamber of Commerce, P.O. Box 258, Chincoteague, VA 23336 (804-336-6161), or stop by their office at 6733 Maddox Boulevard. The building is in the middle of a traffic circle between the town and Assateague Island.

For information about some of the publications and references available on this fascinating area, write for the mail-order sales catalog of the nonprofit Chincoteague Natural History Association, P.O. Box 971, Chincoteague, VA 23336. Their brochure contains books on the area's history, birds, wildlife, wetlands, and vegetation, along with books designed for children and for teachers. Enclose a self-addressed stamped envelope.

At the Maryland end of Assateague Island is the Barrier Island Visitor Center, with exhibits, an aquarium, and maps.

The National Aeronautics and Space Administration (NASA) has a visitors center on State 175, which you will pass on your way to the islands. NASA experimental rockets and satellites of the National Oceanic and Atmospheric Administration (NOAA) are launched here from Wallops Island. If your timing is fortuitous, you might get to see a spectacular night launch light up the sky along the Atlantic seaboard.

Where: East of Chincoteague Island, off northern end of Eastern Shore peninsula. From US 13, take State 175 east to islands.

Hours: Open daily year-round: 5:00 A.M. to 10:00 P.M. May to September, 6:00 A.M. to 8:00 P.M. April and October, 6:00 A.M. to 6:00 P.M. November to March. After-hours surf fishing by permit.

Admission: Small fee.

Best time to visit: All year for bird-watching and wildlife. Easter weekend for annual Decoy and Arts Festival. Last Wednesday and Thursday of July for pony-penning and auction. Late November for Assateague Island Waterfowl Week.

Activities Bird-watching, wildlife observation, beach and trail hiking, bicycling, lifeguarded beach, interpretive programs, amphitheater, saltwater fishing, crabbing, shellfishing, two visitors centers. Campgrounds nearby. Wheelchair access to all public buildings; access ramp to ocean at main beach parking lot.

Concessions: Wildlife tours (reservations at visitors center).

Pets: Not allowed in refuge or in Assateague State Park in Maryland.

For more information:

Refuge Manager, Chincoteague National Wildlife Refuge, P.O. Box 62, Chincoteague, VA 23336 (804-336-6122).

For specific information about naturalist or beach recreation activities, call Tom's Cove Visitor Center (804-336-6577).

To find out about activities on the Maryland end of the island, call Assateague State Park, Route 611, 7307 Stephen Decatur Highway, Berlin, MD 21811 (410-641-2120).

CHIPPOKES PLANTATION STATE PARK

Chippokes Plantation State Park gracefully combines history and recreation at this 1,400-acre site along the south bank of the James River across from Jamestown island.

Pronounced CHIP-oaks, the estate was named for a friendly Native American chief. The plantation was established in 1619 and is the oldest continually farmed property in the country. The age of Chippokes is evident in the elegant, well-kept mansion, as well as the trees and shrubs on the grounds. More than a mile of tall cedars line the driveway, and massive oaks shade the formal gardens around the house.

Visit the Farm and Forestry Museum and sawmill exhibit on the estate to learn how farming practices of the 1600s are still used today.

But if you just want to enjoy the park for its outdoors, there are four miles of hiking trails and three miles of bike trails, a modern visitors center and swimming complex, and picnic tables overlooking the wide James River.

The Pork, Peanut and Pine Festival held on the grounds in mid-July not only offers all the usual magnets of Chippokes, but adds good pork barbecue, peanut pie, and other homemade foods, hay rides and farm exhibits. While you're sampling the food, you can stroll through the high-quality arts and crafts show that sprawls over the open lawn and winds along sun-dappled pathways beneath the oak canopy.

A piece of good news—development of new campgrounds for the park is in the works. In the past, we've searched hard for a place to camp on the south side of the river, with no luck.

Also, nearby Surry has a motel and bed and breakfast. Or, for a modest fee and rarely more than a half-hour wait, you can take the ferry at Surry for a short but scenic trip across the James River to campgrounds on the other side. Our favorite is First Settlers Campground, just off the ferry on the right, with its beautiful shaded campsites, many of them at water's edge. Bring insect repellent. Call 804-229-4900 for more information.

Or you can drive a few miles farther to Williamsburg, which is overflowing with restaurants, motels, and hotels.

Where: Surry County on James River. From Surry, take State 10 east, go left on County 634 and follow the signs.

Hours: Park and trails 8:00 A.M. until dusk daily, year-round. Mansion open Memorial Day weekend to Labor Day, Garden Week, and Christmas season.

Admission: Small parking fee, admission fee to mansion and pool fee.

Best time to visit: Spring for formal gardens. Early December for decorated mansion. Mid-July for Pork, Peanut and Pine Festival, which celebrates area industries.

Activities: Tour of mansion and formal gardens, Farm and Forestry Museum and sawmill exhibit, hiking, bicycle trails, self-guiding trails, picnic shelters, pool, saltwater fishing, visitors center, interpretive programs, playground. Most areas wheelchair accessible.

Concessions: Snack bar.

Pets: Must be on leash. Not allowed in pool area or inside buildings.

Other: Famous Smithfield country ham, from hogs raised on peanuts (ask at the park). Ferry at Surry crosses James River to Colonial Williamsburg and Jamestown island.

For more information:

Chippokes Plantation State Park, 695 Chippokes Park Road, Surry, VA 23883. (804-294-3625 or 804-786-1712).

THE GREAT DISMAL SWAMP

The Great Dismal Swamp isn't so dismal at all. It depends on what you're looking for.

If it's the twentieth-century fast lane with booming night clubs and crowded sidewalks, then the resort city of Virginia Beach less than thirty miles to the northeast is your cup of tea.

But if you like bears, snakes, history, wading birds, cypress knees, and ghost stories, then the Great Dismal Swamp will enchant you, just as it has Native Americans as well as European settlers and their descendants since its discovery.

George Washington surveyed it, dug mammoth ditches, and tried to drain it. Loggers over the centuries hauled its rich native cypress logs to market, and runaway slaves used its miles of trackless wilderness to shake off dogs and men. Sailing ships carried the swamp's dark water on long sea voyages because the tannin in the water kept it fresh.

The Dismal Swamp Canal is the country's oldest man-made canal still in use today and has been placed on the National Register of Historic Places. The canal is also a National Historic Civil Engineering Landmark and is part of the Atlantic Intracoastal Waterway. Beautiful pleasure boats traveling to and from Florida use the canal daily.

One of the last private owners of the Great Dismal Swamp was Union Camp Corporation, which in 1973 donated 49,100 acres of the swamp to The Nature Conservancy to hold in trust. A year later, The Nature Conservancy donated the land to the U.S. Department of the Interior to establish the Great Dismal Swamp National Wildlife Refuge, which today consists of 107,000 acres of forested wetlands that have been greatly altered by drainage and repeated logging.

Lake Drummond

A shallow natural lake in the heart of the swamp, Lake Drummond contributes to the mystery of the place. Drummond is one of only two natural lakes in the state. The other is Mountain Lake at the opposite end of Virginia.

No one knows how Lake Drummond was formed. Native Americans on the coast told early English settlers that a "firebird" caused it. The legend set off speculation that a meteorite came flaming through the atmosphere and buried itself in the soft muck of the swamp. If so, it left a 3,100-acre crater that eventually filled with water.

Today, although Lake Drummond is open for fishing year-round, the fishing isn't very good because of the high acidic content of the swamp. However, the lake at least provides the obligatory ghost story about an ethereal lady in a white canoe. She is reputed to cruise the lake's dark waters when the moon and tide are right.

Several unpaved roads offer hikers and bicyclists opportunities to see wildlife and wildflowers. The best of these roads, with the shortest trek to Lake Drummond, is the four- to five-mile Washington Ditch Road. It begins just north of the refuge headquarters on the west side of the swamp, off County 642. The mile-long, self-guided Boardwalk Trail on the Washington Ditch Road gives hikers a good idea of what the swamp is all about.

No spot in Virginia can offer the variety of wildlife that lives in this expansive land-water wilderness. George Washington called the Great Dismal Swamp a "glorious paradise" for wildlife in his time. Nothing has changed. Among the more common species are white-tailed deer, black bear, bobcat, fox, raccoon, otter, opossum, numerous snakes (including the poisonous cottonmouth moccasin), wild turkey, great blue heron, osprey, and a variety of ducks. In winter, hunters splash through the swamp outside the refuge behind long-legged hounds as both men and dogs follow black bear. (Hunting with dogs is not permitted on refuge land.)

Birds and Flowers

Countless numbers of migrating birds pass through in spring and fall. The peak of spring migration in the refuge is mid-April to mid-May. A total of 209 bird species have been identified, including 35 species of warblers. Some unusual sightings include the Kentucky warbler, Wilson's warbler, sora, king rail, and bald eagle.

Those who enjoy wildflowers also come to the Great Dismal Swamp. In the middle of March, out of winter's drab remains springs the dwarf trillium. Then come orchids, coral honeysuckle, and yellow jessamine. Silky camellia begin flowering in late May.

Whereas the colors of spring are soft and subtle, the colors of autumn are brilliant, peaking from late October to late November.

The one campground in the swamp is operated by the U.S. Army Corps of Engineers at Lake Drummond and is accessible only by boat. Canoes and small boats can navigate the Feeder Ditch to the campground. Boats must be small enough to portage around the water-control structure near the lake. Boat motors are limited to ten horsepower. The launch ramp to the Dismal Swamp Canal and Feeder Ditch is on US 17, about three miles north of the Virginia state line. The campground is open year-round and has a boat-mooring pier, campfire areas, grills, picnic tables, and screened-in sheds with tables. There are also comfort stations with water hookups, which are closed from December to March.

If you haven't spent a night here before, it's a good idea to check with the campground for suggestions about what to carry in with you. Biting insects can be a problem in warm weather. Come prepared. You can't just jump in your car when you realize you don't have your insect repellent.

Where: South of Norfolk in southeastern Virginia and northeastern North Carolina.
Hours: Daily from half hour before sunrise to half hour after

Black-eyed Susans

sunset. Washington Ditch entrance 6:30 A.M. to 8:00 P.M. daily, April 1 to September 30; 6:30 A.M. to 5:00 P.M. daily, October 1 to March 31.

Admission: No fees for the boat launch on US 17 or campground.

Best time to visit: Anytime for hiking, bicycling. Early May for migrating songbirds. Spring through fall for wildlife observation.

Activities: Hiking, bicycling, photography, wildlife observation, fishing, boating, primitive boat-in camping.

Concessions: None.

Pets: Must be under owner's control at campground and on a leash in refuge.

Other: Parts of refuge are closed in fall for controlled deer hunt.

For more information:

Dismal Swamp Canal Visitor/Welcome Center, 2356 North Highway 17, South Mills, NC 27976 (919-771-8333).

Lake Drummond Campground (804-421-7401).

Refuge Manager, Great Dismal Swamp National Wildlife Refuge, P.O. Box 349, Suffolk, VA 23439-0349 (804-986-3705).

KIPTOPEKE STATE PARK

Try this in the fall at Kiptopeke (pronounced KIP-toe-peek). Stand on the broad earthen fishing pier that juts into Chesapeake Bay. Watch the way the setting sun catches the row of sunken World War II ships just out of casting distance.

The old concrete—yes, concrete—ships carried war matériel more than half a century ago. Now they sit on the bottom of the shallow bay, their vast gray sides stained with leakage from metal portholes. The nine ships are lined bow to stern to protect the fishing pier and the park's beaches from the relentless chop and erosion of the Chesapeake.

The spacious lighted fishing pier offers unusual access to

more than twenty species of saltwater fish. If you thread a blood-worm or a piece of shrimp on a hook, it's likely that you'll catch a couple of flounder or pan-sized gray trout (weakfish) for supper. Especially in fall.

But the most unusual thing you can do when autumn winds come sweeping across the Chesapeake is to take part in the nationally famous bird-trapping and banding that are held at Kiptopeke State Park each September and October. The finger of land known as the Eastern Shore of Virginia (also called the Delmarva Peninsula) is a major fall migratory route for many species of songbirds as well as hawks and other birds of prey. The birds funnel south down the shores of the Chesapeake and stop briefly in or near Kiptopeke State Park for food and a breather before launching themselves across the bay or upon the trackless Atlantic Ocean. Kiptopeke, one of Virginia's newest parks, is fortuitously located near the tip of the peninsula.

The bird-banding at Kiptopeke has been going on each fall for more than thirty years. Tiny warblers, vireos, tanagers, flycatchers, downy woodpeckers, redstarts, and yellowthroats by the thousands are caught in almost-invisible but harmless mist nets. The nets are set along trails and thickets among the sand dunes.

Once trapped, each bird is equipped with a tiny leg band and released. Some are caught year after year. The banding program is a project of the Virginia Society of Ornithology with help from volunteers and the nongame and endangered species program of the Virginia Department of Game and Inland Fisheries.

Bird-watchers also gather at Kiptopeke State Park each September and October for the annual hawk migration south along the shore of Chesapeake Bay. The Hawk Migration Association of America estimates that as many as 30,000 hawks, falcons, and occasional eagles pass by Kiptopeke during the peak migration between mid-September and mid-October.

Birding and hawk-watching have gotten so popular with

visitors that an annual Eastern Shore Birding Festival is held in October. It attracts several thousand people during an early October weekend each year. Tours are arranged for the state park, nearby Eastern Shore of Virginia National Wildlife Refuge, The Nature Conservancy's Virginia Coast Reserve, Mockhorn Wildlife Management Area, and the islands of the Chesapeake Bay Bridge–Tunnel complex.

Headquarters for the festival is Sunset Beach Inn (804-331-4786), located south of Kiptopeke State Park, near the north end of the Chesapeake Bay Bridge–Tunnel.

Across US 13 from the inn are 651 acres set aside to protect migratory and endangered species and for wildlife-oriented recreation. Established in 1984, the Eastern Shore of Virginia National Wildlife Refuge consists of maritime forest, myrtle and bayberry thickets, grasslands, croplands, and fresh and brackish ponds.

After a stop at the visitors center, take the half-mile interpretive trail loop through woods, past an old graveyard and to a World War II bunker. The structure once housed sixteen-inch guns designed to protect navy installations across the mouth of the bay in Virginia Beach and Norfolk. From atop the bunker, you will have a wide view of the refuge marshes, barrier islands, bays and inlets, and Atlantic Ocean.

Spring brings marsh and shorebirds to the refuge, including glossy ibises, willets, and cattle egrets. Bobwhite call from the fields. Wood ducks and bluebirds make use of nest boxes.

In summer, you might be lucky enough to see an osprey returning to its nest atop a refuge-built platform, a pair of river otters diving for fish, a clapper rail or black-crowned night heron in tall marsh grasses, or, as you leave at dusk, a racoon or red fox scurrying across the path.

In fall and winter, northern harriers fly low over the marshes, and American kestrels hover in fields above their prey.

Listen for the call of snow geese and tundra swans coming to feed in planted fields at dawn, or returning to the protected water of an inlet at sunset.

Year-round residents include black ducks, great blue herons, great horned owls, screech owls, woodpeckers, warblers, and a variety of other songbirds.

About 300 bird species have been identified at the refuge. Half that many were recorded in the area in a single Christmas Bird Count—one of the highest counts north of Florida. More American woodcock were tallied here than anywhere in the United States during the Christmas Bird Count of 1993.

Where: Park is off US 13 on Eastern Shore peninsula, three miles north of Chesapeake Bay Bridge–Tunnel. From US 13, turn west on County 704 and go half mile to park entrance. Refuge is off US 13, one mile north of bridge-tunnel. From US 13, turn east on County 600.

Hours: Park swimming beach, interpretive programs, Labor Day to Memorial Day. Campground, spring through late November. Walking and bicycle trails, fishing pier year-round; pier lighted all night during summer season. Bird-banding in September and October. Refuge open dawn to dusk, year-round.

Admission: Small parking fee for park. Full-service-campground fee. Refuge is free. (Bay bridge–tunnel toll is $10.00 each way. You can avoid bridge and toll by coming from north.)

Best time to visit: September and October for bird-banding. Anytime for walking trails (bring insect repellent).

Activitites: Park has picnicking, beach swimming, camping, bicycling, outstanding saltwater surf and pier fishing, bird-banding, nature trails with boardwalks, observation tower, viewing concrete ships from World War II. Refuge has half-mile interpretive trail, wildlife observation, visitors center.

Concessions: Vending machines in park.

Pets: Must be on leash.
For more information:
Kiptopeke State Park, 3540 Kiptopeke Drive, Cape Charles, VA 23310 (804-331-2267 or 804-786-1712).
Refuge Manager, Eastern Shore of Virginia National Wildlife Refuge, RFD 1, Box 122B, Cape Charles, VA 23310-9725 (804-331-2760).

LEESYLVANIA STATE PARK

Leesylvania, one of Virginia's newest state parks, is the ancestral home of the famous Lee family of Virginia and home of Robert E. Lee's father. Chief Ranger Brendon Hanafin calls the park a natural oasis in urban northern Virginia, located as it is along the Potomac River and Occoquan Bay. It's a good place to see ducks, geese, swans, eagles, osprey, kingfishers, and many other birds that like rivers and marshes.

A wide expanse of marsh just opposite the park entrance on Neabsco Road was full of migrating waterfowl one fall morning when we arrived. Our binoculars came in handy.

As you explore Leesylvania's open areas and wooded forests, a white-tailed deer may raise its flaglike tail and bolt out of your path. If something swims out from the water's edge as you approach, making a V-shaped trail across the water, it is likely a beaver or muskrat. Given the variety of woodpeckers, hawks, waterfowl, and songbirds here, you will find a bird identification book helpful.

The park has a boat-launching area with a store and snack bar nearby. Passage of a recent bond referendum for the Department of Conservation and Recreation gave Leesylvania more than $4 million for improvements. New attractions will include a visitors center and upgrading of the amphitheater and picnic area.

The current picnic area has a long natural sand beach, but

no swimming is allowed because of unhealthy water quality, bottom hazards, and boating traffic.

While you're here, take a hike into the past on Lee's Woods Historical Trail, beginning at the end of the park road at the cul-de-sac. But first be sure to get a free copy of the well-written illustrated trail guide "A Potomac Legacy" in the box at the trail-head (or ask a ranger for it). Biting insects are sometimes a nuisance. Bring repellent.

Where: Northern Virginia between Woodbridge and Fredericks-burg, on Potomac River. From US 1, take County 610 (Neabsco Road) east two miles.

Hours: 8:00 a.m until dusk daily, year-round.

Admission: Small parking fee. Boat-launching fee.

Best time to visit: Anytime for hiking. Spring and fall for nature programs, fishing.

Activities: Day use only. Hiking, historic interpretive trail, guided nature walks and canoe tours, boat launch (including motorboats), freshwater fishing, picnicking. Some handicapped facilities.

Concessions: Seasonal store and snack bar.

Pets: Must be on leash.

Although Leesylvania is for day use only, you can camp at a nearby national park, Prince William Forest Park. Developed by the Civilian Conservation Corps in the 1930s, the park has a visitors center, extensive hiking trails, and wooded campsites with picnic tables and fire grates. No showers or hookups are provided. Entrance fee and camping fee apply. The park entrance is located north of County 619, just west of the Triangle exit of I-95.

For more information:

Leesylvania State Park, 16236 Neabsco Road, Wood-bridge, VA 22191 (703-670-0372 or 804-786-1712).

Prince William Forest Park, P.O. Box 209, Triangle, VA 22172-0209 (703-221-7181).

MASON NECK

It rained the night before we arrived at Mason Neck State Park. The leaf-strewn path of the Bay View Nature Trail was quiet underfoot. We walked up on two deer and a squirrel before they saw us, and surprised a great blue heron fishing at the edge of Belmont Bay.

The time was late fall. As is often the case in the off-season, we practically had the park and wildlife refuge to ourselves. A lone, wiry, middle-aged man in a wet suit launched a small and fragile-looking sailboat on Belmont Bay. His craft caught the wind and became smaller and smaller as he drifted far away.

Later we saw another man with two energetic boxers on leashes. It was difficult to tell whether man or dogs were in charge. As we came off the self-guiding nature trail, a young man and woman, each with a child in a back carrier, were just heading out.

Except for these folks and a helpful park ranger who stopped to chat from his truck, the park this day was left to wildlife, to sun reflecting off the American holly, to the gentle breeze.

The Mason Neck peninsula, just south of Washington, D.C., is bordered on the north by Pohick Bay. To the southeast is the Potomac River. Add Occoquan and Belmont Bays to the southwest, and northern Virginia residents and visitors have a fine outdoor getaway from busy schedules and congested highways.

Drive down the tree-lined road at the entrance to Mason Neck State Park and Wildlife Refuge. Walk the refuge trail under a canopy of beech, hickory, and oak. You might spot a soaring bald eagle along the open waters of Belmont Bay. While enjoying the place, take time to think about the hard work of a determined woman some thirty years ago to save this piece of the natural world.

After learning of a plan to develop a city here in the sixties, Elizabeth Hartwell formed a committee to encourage the acquisition of land by private and public agencies that would save the bald eagle habitat on this peninsula. That marvelous rescuer of habitat, The Nature Conservancy, purchased land, followed by the Virginia Department of Conservation and Recreation, the Northern Virginia Regional Park Authority, and the U.S. Fish and Wildlife Service.

In a fine example of interagency cooperation, more than 5,000 acres have been set aside in Mason Neck Wildlife Refuge, Mason Neck State Park, Gunston Hall Plantation, and Pohick Bay Regional Park for ecological, historical, and recreational value.

The facilities complement one another. Composed of bay shore, tidal marsh, and mature hardwood forest, the peninsula is a haven for many kinds of animal and plant life. Although there's no camping at the state park, year-round camping (along with many other activities) is available at nearby Pohick Bay Regional Park.

Between the two parks is Gunston Hall Plantation, National Historic Landmark and eighteenth-century home of statesman George Mason, one of Virginia's founding fathers. There you can wander through the restored Colonial mansion, formal gardens, nature trail, and deer park.

Where: From I-95 or US 1 north of Woodbridge and south of Washington, D.C., follow State 242 east about three miles to Pohick Bay Regional Park and another mile to Mason Neck National Wildlife Refuge and Mason Neck State Park. Gunston Hall is off State 242 between the two parks.

Hours: State park, 8:00 A.M. until dusk daily, year-round. Wildlife refuge, dawn to dusk, year-round. (State park and refuge closed for two weeks in early November for controlled deer hunt.) Pohick Bay, closes at dark (park and campgrounds open year-round). Gunston Hall, 9:30 A.M. to 5:00 P.M., year-round except Thanksgiving, Christmas, and New Year's Day.

Admission: State park, small parking fee. Wildlife refuge, free. Pohick Bay, entrance fee for out-of-area residents, camping fee. Gunston Hall, admission fee.

Best time to visit: State park, winter and spring for eagles; spring through fall for interpretive programs, wildlife observation, boating; anytime for hiking. Wildlife refuge, winter and spring for eagles, spring and fall for bird-banding and wildlife observation, anytime for hiking. Pohick Bay, Memorial Day weekend to Labor Day for water activities; anytime for camping, hiking, fishing. Gunston Hall, anytime.

Activities: State park, picnicking, hiking, self-guided nature trail with boardwalks over marshes, saltwater fishing, boating (car-top launch), seasonal visitors center, environmental education center, interpretive programs. Wildlife refuge has hiking, wildlife observation; seasonal group tours and outdoor classroom programs for teachers by prior arrangement. Photo blind available on permit basis. Pohick Bay has year-round camping, saltwater pier fishing and boat ramp, nature trail, observation deck, seasonal swimming pool, challenging golf course, minigolf, frisbee golf, picnic shelters, bridle trail, sailboat and paddleboat rental, boat storage. Gunston Hall has mansion tour, formal gardens, nature trail, picnic area.

Concessions: State park and wildlife refuge have none. Pohick Bay has seasonal snack bar, camp store. Gunston Hall has gift shop.

Pets: Must be on leash in parks, in refuge, and on grounds of Gunston Hall. Not permitted in Gunston Hall mansion.

Other: State park has seasonal canoe trips on marshes of Kanes

Creek. Seasonal children's programs. Wildlife refuge has bald eagle and heron rookery.

For more information:

Mason Neck State Park, 7301 High Point Road, Lorton, VA 22079; 703-550-0362 (visitors center), 703-550-0960 (office), or 804-786-1712.

Mason Neck Wildlife Refuge, 14344 Jeff Davis Highway, Woodbridge, VA 22191 (703-690-1297).

Pohick Bay Regional Park, Lorton, VA 22079 (703-339-6100) or write c/o Northern Virginia Regional Park Authority, 5400 Ox Road, Fairfax Station, VA 22039 (703-352-5900 or 703-339-6104).

Gunston Hall, Mason Neck, Lorton, VA 22079 (703-550-9220).

MOUNT VERNON TRAIL

The eighteen-mile Mount Vernon Trail connects America's past and present. The trail extends from George Washington's home at Mount Vernon in Fairfax County north along the Potomac River, through Old Town Alexandria, to Theodore Roosevelt Island. The northern end of the trail, which lies across the water from the Lincoln Memorial in Washington, D.C., connects with rougher Arlington County trails.

Running parallel to the Mount Vernon Trail is the George Washington Memorial Parkway. Between the two, you can drive, bicycle, run, or walk through little-known pieces of Virginia's and America's past.

If you decide to drive, allow time to park along the way and take some of the side trails. It would be a shame to miss the Potomac breezes in the red maples, oaks, sumac, and hickory trees. Or to miss the great variety of marsh birds' and songbirds' calls, coming from the willows, birches and elders along the banks. In spring and fall, you may catch a glimpse of tiny migrating warblers busily searching for insects in the riverbank shrubbery. The parula warbler, with a blue back and yellow throat, and the yellow warbler, with a yellow breast and yellow tail spots, are two likely candidates.

Both the drive and the walk are beautiful in spring, when

A red fox

dogwood and azalea bloom. Though you may think you're in the heart of a metropolis, you may be observed from the undergrowth by white-tailed deer, raccoon, wild turkey, or maybe even a shy red fox.

For a brochure about the historical significance of the places linked by the parkway and trail, and a map showing points of interest, rest rooms, boat launches, restaurants, and parking areas, contact the Superintendent, George Washington Memorial Parkway, Turkey Run Park, McLean, VA 22101 (703-285-2598).

Points of Interest:

Fort Hunt Park — About three miles north of Mount Vernon, accessible by Fort Hunt Road off Vernon View Drive, are 156 acres of park for picnicking, hiking, birding, or just resting after walking the Mount Vernon Trail. Across the Potomac to the east is Fort Washington, strategically placed to defend the capital in the early nineteenth century.

River Farm — This twenty-seven-acre farm was one of five farms on the Potomac between Mount Vernon and Alexandria owned by George Washington. Now the headquarters of the American Horticultural Society, the farm features rose gardens, water gardens, a ballroom yard, woodland walk, and other test and display collections. Several children's theme collections, such as an alphabet garden, a dinosaur garden, a jungle garden, and a butterfly garden, make it a fun place to bring the family.

Open 8:30 A.M. to 5:00 P.M. Monday to Friday except major holidays. Located on the river side of the Memorial Parkway just south of the stone bridge on Alexandria Avenue. River Farm, 7931 East Boulevard Drive, Alexandria, VA 22308-1300 (703-768-5700).

Dyke Marsh — Where jetliners roar overhead and within sight of the I-95 bridge is the Dyke Marsh, a 240-acre wetland with estuary habitat typical of the Potomac. More than 250 species of birds have been identified here. A side trail just north of Belle View Boulevard leads into the marsh. On the north end of the marsh is a picnic area called Belle Haven, formerly the name of a settlement of Scottish merchants, and Belle Haven Marina, where you can launch your boat, rent a sailboat, and sign up for sailing lessons.

Jones Point Lighthouse — A favored fishing and picnicking spot, at the I-95 Woodrow Wilson Bridge and the southern edge of Old Town Alexandria, this small lighthouse warned of nearby sandbars from 1836 to 1925.

Alexandria — As you pass through the old-town area of this former center of tobacco trading and shipbuilding, you will see hundreds of restored eighteenth- and nineteenth-century homes and public buildings.

Daingerfield Island — Just south of the Washington National Airport is this 107-acre peninsula (technically not an island anymore). Hiking, bird-watching, and picnicking are popular here. A full-service sailboat marina and a restaurant with a view of the D.C. skyline are on the northern end of the peninsula.

Theodore Roosevelt Island — Explore the 2.5 miles of trails through the marsh, swamp, and upland forest of this eighty-eight-acre natural area in the Potomac under the I-66 bridge to Constitution Avenue in Washington. Open daily 8:00 A.M. until dark.

Great Falls Park — To get to this 800-acre natural area, where you can witness what happens to a wide river forced into a narrow gorge, take I-495 south from the northern end of the George Washington Memorial Parkway and go north on the Old Georgetown Pike (State 193). A right turn on County 738 will take you to the visitors center.

The Great Falls of the Potomac attract both tourists and local residents who enjoy the roar of water charging over a steep wall and tumbling over boulders. Hiking, climbing, fishing, and picnicking are available from 9:00 A.M. until dark daily, year-round (except Christmas).

Of special interest is the moderately strenuous 2.5-mile River Trail, from the picnic area along Mather Gorge to Cow Hoof Rock and a dramatic view of the gorge. Guided walks are conducted all year. An entrance fee is charged. Call 703-285-2966 for more information.

NORFOLK BOTANICAL GARDEN

If you've got spring fever, the Norfolk Botanical Garden may have just the fix you need.

Come April, one of the largest collections of azaleas, other rhododendrons, camellias, and roses on the East Coast will put a visual end to winter in a fantastic display of color.

Since its inception in 1938, the botanical garden has earned a reputation for its azaleas, attracting thousands of visitors to the annual International Azalea Festival each spring, when a coronation ceremony is held for Queen Azalea and her court. During the festival, the garden also salutes the North Atlantic Treaty Organization (NATO) with performing and cultural arts presentations by NATO countries.

But there's more to the story. Among the native plants in the natural setting covering 155 acres are many specialized gardens. You can stroll along twelve miles of paved pathways, through the Renaissance Garden, with its symmetrical grassy terraces. Walk

WHAT'S BLOOMING WHEN
January: camellias, witch hazel, tropical greenhouse plants
February: wintersweet, camellias, pansies, daphne
March: camellias, daffodils, *Pieris japonica*, magnolias
April: tulips, azaleas, dogwood
May: rhododendrons, roses, azaleas
June: oleander, hydrangea, daylilies, roses
July: crape myrtle, annuals, hibiscus
August–September: annuals, roses, crape myrtle
October–December: roses, camellias, wintersweet

through rose arboretums and inhale the heady aroma of a quarter million rose blooms in the Bicentennial Rose Garden. Wander by the tranquil Japanese Garden, the Sunken Garden, and up the steps for a panoramic view from the Hill of Nations Observation Tower.

The City of Norfolk and the Tidewater District of the Virginia Federation of Garden Clubs financed the planting of a Fragrance Garden for the blind in 1963, and it was made accessible with ramp entrances, braille markers, and handrails.

From spring through Labor Day, canal boats take visitors along quiet waterways through the gardens for a different perspective. There's also a trackless train if you'd like to ride. If you plan to take the train or boat, we recommend leaving time to walk in at least part of the garden for a more personal experience, in case you really do want to stop and smell the flowers. We sat on a bench to watch a kingfisher dive for fish in one of the garden canals—something we couldn't have done on the train.

Also, if you just couldn't fit your treadmill in the car on this trip, you'll never find a more pleasant place for an aerobic walk than the paths of this botanical garden. Many area residents feel lucky to have their daily exercise route surrounded by cultivated natural beauty.

Lake Whitehurst, at the garden entrance, is a popular resting and feeding area for waterfowl. Although vehicles are not allowed to pull over on the causeway, just past the entrance booth on the left is a picnic area that borders the lake, where you can watch the ducks, geese, and wading birds.

In winter, boats and trains are stored away. Azaleas and roses are dormant. An alluring quiet and peace settles over the garden, as most life waits beneath the soil for spring. Winter visitors can still enjoy the climate-controlled Tropical Pavilion, with 3,600 square feet housing 100 plant species from equatorial regions of the world. Garden of Lights, a $300,000 holiday light project, is presented nightly from Thanksgiving to New Year's Eve.

Workshops, symposiums, and special events such as outdoor concerts, outdoor sculpture and art exhibitions, and plant sales are scheduled throughout the year.

Where: Adjacent to Norfolk International Airport. From I-64, take exit 279 (Norview Avenue) north. Turn left on Azalea Garden Road and look for entrance on right.

Hours: 8:30 A.M. until sunset daily, year-round. Train tours daily from mid-March to October, boat tours daily from mid-April to Labor Day, weather permitting.

Admission: Small entrance fee (children under five, free), small fee for train and boat tours.

Best time to visit: April to June for azaleas, May for rhododendrons, mid-May to October for roses, September to March for camellias and hollies. Anytime for walking, enjoying landscape, picnicking.

Activities: Walking, picnicking, gift shop, train and boat tours, observation tower, educational programs, special events.

Concession: Gift shop, teahouse, train and boat tours.

Pets: Not allowed.

For more information:

Norfolk Botanical Garden, Azalea Garden Road, Norfolk, VA 23518 (804-640-6879 or 804-441-5830).

NORTHERN VIRGINIA REGIONAL PARKS

Northern Virginia, or that portion of it adjacent to the District of Columbia, has seen phenomenal growth in recent years. People continue to move farther and farther away from the District of Columbia to escape suburban sprawl. More malls are built to serve them, and more expressways are constructed for commuters to get back to their jobs in the nation's capital.

Small towns struggle to keep their identities. Instead of the usual bordering farms, meadows, and dirt roads, towns are elbowed by shopping centers and bumped up to cul-de-sacs.

Thoughtful people saw what was happening, and were alarmed. They realized that the doe no longer brought her new fawns to drink each summer from the little stream out back. And the red fox no longer occasionally dined on one of the old farmer's chickens. Bluebirds and meadowlarks no longer sang from the fence in the neighbor's field.

In fact, where was the field itself? As for the stream, it was diverted into a culvert beneath a parking lot. The farmer's land was sold at auction—for a new office complex.

With the help of some generous donors, a group of concerned citizens began work more than thirty-five years ago to save corners of natural beauty from the bulldozer. The group, which became the Northern Virginia Regional Park Authority (NVRPA), gradually set aside more than 10,000 acres of woodland, waters, meadows, and trails—even one wilderness—for city-weary folks to enjoy.

Although recreation and playgrounds are the emphasis at some of the parks, where the big attractions are the water slide, the wave pool, golf courses, and ballfields, the parks we mention here are of special interest for their natural beauty and value to wildlife.

Washington and Old Dominion Railroad
Regional Park (W&OD Trail)

The Washington and Old Dominion Railroad Regional Park was named for the railroad that operated from 1859 to 1968 between the nation's capital and the Blue Ridge Mountains. The old railroad bed was a natural as a recreation area for those who like a change of scenery when they walk or ride bicycles or horses. Nicknamed the W&OD Trail, this is one of the new "linear" parks—only 100 feet wide but forty-five miles long.

From its start in Arlington County (at Shirlington Road and Four Mile Run Drive), the paved right-of-way takes foot or bicycle travelers from an urban surrounding, through Falls Church and then Vienna, gradually becoming suburban and finally rural as it gets into Loudoun County and heads for its western end at Purcellville.

The trail may be accessed where it crosses highways. There is a parking area in Vienna near the trail's junction with Church Street and Mill Street. From Vienna west, a gravel bridle path parallels the asphalt for thirty miles to the trail's end.

After Vienna, the trail passes through Reston and Herndon. You can wave hello to Sterling residents working in flower and vegetable gardens on the north side of the trail. Then you'll come to the State 28 access (parking area nearby), two to three miles south of State 7.

From State 28 west, the trail leads through fields and farmlands, over streams and by woodlands. It passes a couple of blocks south of historic downtown Leesburg before proceeding to its end at Twenty-first Street in Purcellville.

We recommend the more western reaches of the trail for scenery and to avoid congestion. It's wise to walk with a partner and plan your route so you'll be finished before dark. Use common sense to avoid startling a horse or hiker when you come from behind. Be sure to obey stop signs at road crossings. Many conscientious trail users help keep the path beautiful by picking up trash and carrying it to the next receptacle. For a colorful trail

A bluebird

guide showing fast-food restaurants, bicycle shops, and rest rooms along the way, contact the Northern Virginia Regional Park Authority.

Where: Northern Virginia, from Arlington to Purcellville.
Hours: Dawn to dusk. Do not use W&OD at night.
Admission: No charge.
Best time to visit: Anytime.
Activities: Hiking, running, bicycling, horseback riding, fitness stations.
Concessions: Nearby.
Pets: Must be on leash or otherwise restrained.
Other: The park connects a series of wayside parks and other trails. Contact Northern Virginia Regional Park Authority for more information.
For more information:
      W&OD Railroad Regional Park, 21293 Smiths Switch Road, Ashburn, VA 22011 (703-729-0596).
      Northern Virginia Regional Park Authority, 5400 Ox Road, Fairfax Station, VA 22039 (703-352-5900).

The Bull Run–Occoquan Trail

Through seventeen miles of stream valley along Bull Run and Occoquan Reservoir in Fairfax County is the Bull Run–Occoquan Trail (BROT). Traversing marshes and tributary streams, descending into deep ravines, and climbing wooded hillsides, this path connects 5,000 acres of parkland and provides a valuable wildlife corridor.

      At the northern terminus of the BROT is Bull Run Regional Park, where numerous birds and animals find protection. Lying in your tent at dawn, you may hear the sharp gobble of a wild turkey looking for a mate, or the soft cooing of a mourning dove. Don't be surprised if a covey of startled quail flushes suddenly at your feet as you cross a meadow. If you hear a raucous cackling and turn your head to see a huge crested woodpecker attach itself to the side of a sycamore, it's probably the pileated—the one that provided the inspiration for Woody Woodpecker.

In early spring in Bull Run Regional Park you can see a carpet of wetland bluebells and other wildflowers. Follow portions of the trails with white and yellow blazes through the forest swamp.

Stop in at the park's visitors center to learn about the Native Americans of the Powhatan Confederacy who once inhabited this stream valley. During the Civil War, Bull Run was a strategic defense line between North and South and was the site of two major battles.

As you follow the blue blazes of the Bull Run–Occoquan Trail toward its southern end at Fountainhead Regional Park, watch also for deer, beaver, squirrel, chipmunk, raccoon, turtles, and the many songbirds, ducks, and geese that live or migrate through here.

Below Fountainhead are two more regional parks: Sandy Run, where calm waters provide a broad, long, straight racing course for rowing crews to practice, and Occoquan, a popular boat-launching spot for fishermen, directly across the water from the town of Occoquan.

In addition to Bull Run Regional Park, the Bull Run–Occoquan Trail is accessible at the following points:

State 28 – From I-66, take State 28 south, pass through the Compton Road intersection, and take the last driveway on the right before crossing the bridge over Bull Run.

Hemlock Overlook Regional Park – In this park, operated jointly by the Northern Virginia Regional Park Authority and George Mason University, only the parking area and trails may be used without permission. All the trails in Hemlock Overlook are steep. From Clifton, take Clifton Road (County 645)

south, then go left on Yates Ford Road (County 615) to the park
entrance.

Bull Run Marina – From State 123, take Clifton Road
(County 645) north to Henderson Road (State 612), then go left
on old Yates Ford Road to the marina. Hemlock-covered slopes,
rock outcroppings, and river islands provide scenery between the
marina and Hemlock Overlook.

Fountainhead Regional Park – From State 123, take
Hampton Road (County 647) north to the park entrance on the
left. Hemlock groves, rhododendron, and pink lady's slippers
cover the steep slopes of the Bull Run–Occoquan Trail. White-
and yellow-blazed trails take you to spectacular overlooks and
hilly terrain.

Where: Northern Virginia, extending twenty-five miles from
Bull Run Regional Park north of Manassas along the Bull Run
and Occoquan River valley to Fountainhead Regional Park, west
of Hampton Road.

Hours: Trail open-year round during daylight hours. Bull Run
Regional Park, Bull Run Marina, and Fountainhead Regional
Park open spring through fall (marina on weekends and holidays
only).

Admission: No charge for trail. Entrance fee for out-of-area
visitors at Bull Run park. Fees for camping, pool, boat launching, and use of other facilities at various parks.

Best time to visit: Anytime for hiking trail or Bull Run shooting
center. Spring through fall for other park activities.

Activities: Hiking, picnicking, wildlife observation on trail. Bull
Run park has shaded campsites with hookups, pool, picnicking,
shooting center (sporting clays, skeet, trap, indoor archery),
minigolf, frisbee golf, children's playground, nature center,
nature trails, bridle paths. Hemlock Overlook has environmental
education center. Bull Run Marina has johnboat and canoe rental,

fishing, picnicking, visitors center. Fountainhead has hiking, fishing, boating (powerboats permitted), picnicking, visitors center, minigolf.

Concessions: Camp store at Bull Run park. Johnboat and canoe rental, tackle shop, snack bar at Bull Run Marina. Tackle shop, boat and motor rental, snack bar at Fountainhead.

Pets: Must be on leash.

Other: Bull Run Country Jamboree (June) and largest All-Breed Dog Show in the United States are held at Bull Run Regional Park. Contact the park authority in late spring for tickets.

For more information:

Northern Virginia Regional Park Authority, 5400 Ox Road, Fairfax Station, VA 22039 (703-352-5900).

Bull Run Regional Park, 7700 Bull Run Drive, Centreville, VA 22020 (703-631-0550).

Hemlock Overlook Regional Park, 13220 Yates Ford Road, Clifton, VA 22024 (703-830-9252).

Bull Run Marina, Old Yates Ford Road, Clifton, VA 22024 (703-830-9252).

Fountainhead Regional Park, 10875 Hampton Road, Fairfax Station, VA 22039 (703-250-9124).

Red Rock Wilderness Overlook Regional Park

Red Rock Wilderness is a natural haven among the hills and woods on the Potomac River east of Leesburg, its sixty-seven acres of land donated as a nature sanctuary.

The quarter-mile trail to the river is relatively flat, but the remaining three miles of trail go up and down steep hills. The reward of taking these trails is the view from overlooks on the high, sheer cliffs. Across the water to the north is Montgomery County, Maryland; on a clear day you can see the distant Blue Ridge foothills to the west.

Where: Loudoun County, 1.5 miles east of Leesburg on County 773, which makes a loop and becomes Fort Evans Road. Look for red rock walls of old buildings at park entrance.
Hours: Daylight hours, year-round. (House is private residence.)
Admission: No entrance fee.
Best time to visit: Anytime.
Activities: Hiking.
Concession: None.
Pets: Must be on leash or otherwise restrained.
For more information:
    Red Rock Wilderness Overlook Regional Park, Edwards Ferry Road, Leesburg, VA 22075 (703-352-5900).

Meadowlark Gardens Regional Park

With a gift of a seventy-five-acre farm, the Northern Virginia Regional Park Authority had the foundation for creating a botanical oasis among old, mature trees and shrubs, near the access road to the Washington-Dulles International Airport.

    In 1987, after the purchase of an additional twenty acres, Meadowlark Gardens opened its gates—a young garden with big ambitions. Each new plant collection added on the hillsides or around one of three lakes brings Meadowlark closer to becoming a world-class garden.

    In early spring, the mockingbird sings from a tall treetop at the edge of the woods that were left intact for wildlife. Flowering cherry trees and Siberian iris decorate Lake Caroline with delicate color. This bloom is followed by the blaze of azaleas in late spring. Bulbs, annuals, and perennials provide more color throughout the year, accented by the cascade of water over a stone dam. The hosta garden, grown for its foliage, is spectacular.

    There are two miles of paved trails, one mile of mulched

trail, and a one-mile perimeter trail. Maps are available at the visitors center.

Where: Fairfax County, between Vienna and Reston. From Vienna, take State 123 to Beulah Road. Go left on Beulah Road to park entrance.
Hours: 10:00 A.M. until about dark daily, year-round. Closed Thanksgiving, Christmas, and New Year's Day.
Admission: No entrance fee.
Best time to visit: Spring through fall.
Activities: Viewing gardens, hiking, bicycling, horseback riding (perimeter trail only), visitors center.
Concessions: Gift shop.
Pets: Only on perimeter trail, on leash.
Other: Horseback riding and bicycling permitted on perimeter trail.
For more information:
    Meadowlark Gardens Regional Park, 9750 Meadowlark Gardens Court, Vienna, VA 22182 (703-255-3631).

SEASHORE STATE PARK AND NATURAL AREA

It is nine o'clock on a raw Sunday morning in January. The wind carries a piquant saltiness from nearby Chesapeake Bay.

Despite the early hour and off-season, the parking lot at the visitors center at Seashore State Park, where most of the hiking and bicycle trails begin, is already one-third full.

There's a reason.

Because of its location near major beaches, its attractive campsites protected by live oak trees, and its unique natural environment, this park gets about one million visitors annually — the most of any park in the Virginia system.

Seashore State Park is divided by US 60, which hugs the

CYPRESS SWAMP

Enter the cypress swamp at Seashore State Park, and you'll do a double take. This is WHERE? South Carolina maybe? Surely not Virginia.

Bald cypress trees, hung gracefully with garlands of Spanish moss, stand knee-deep in dark water—a scene more reminiscent of Charleston or Savannah. You halfway expect to meet Scarlett and Ashley strolling along the path.

Unlike the rest of Virginia, this far southeastern corner of the state is warmed by the Gulf Stream currents, allowing plants and animals more typical of southern climates to survive here.

The cypress tree has a distinctive wide base, which helps to support its root system in the water. The roots send up knobs, called knees, which you may have seen crafted into coffee tables and clocks.

The water is stained with tannin from decaying leaves and wood of the swamp, giving it the color of dark beer.

The swamp is the home of the chicken turtle, one of Virginia's endangered species, with a neck nearly as long as its body. You may also see several species of frogs, woodpeckers, and wading birds on your walk. Look for the little green heron and the snowy egret, slowly and deliberately stalking prey at the water's edge. The area also provides a rest stop for the spring and fall bird migration along the Atlantic flyway.

Chesapeake Bay coastline from the Hampton Roads Bridge–Tunnel to the park. On the Chesapeake Bay side of the road (north side) are 235 campsites, a camp store, and several wheelchair-accessible boardwalks across the dunes to the beach. From the beach you can look across the water to the seventeen-mile-long Chesapeake Bay Bridge–Tunnel, one of the seven modern wonders of the world.

On the south side of US 60 are rental cabins, the visitors center, the environmental education center, and nineteen miles of hiking and bicycle trails through cypress swamps, across a maritime forest sand ridge, over a salt marsh, and into a beech forest. The six-mile Cape Henry Trail ends at a boat-launch facility at the Narrows, a constriction between two inland bays: Broad Bay and Linkhorn Bay. From the banks at the Narrows you may also go saltwater fishing (license required) or crabbing.

If you're planning a summer overnight trip to Seashore State Park, be sure to call ahead for a reservation.

Our most enjoyable stays at this 2,770-acre park have been in spring and fall, when the woods are full of migrating birds. There are a couple of excellent handouts to explain the hiking trails, especially the intriguing Bald Cypress Nature Trail.

Where: Cape Henry in Virginia Beach, where Chesapeake Bay meets the Atlantic. From I-64, take US 13 (at exit 282) north to US 60. Go right on US 60, then right or left on County 343 to enter park.

Hours: Natural area and trails open 8:00 A.M. until dusk, year-round. Campgrounds, store, visitors center, open seasonally (dates may vary annually).

Admission: Small parking fee. Fee for camping, boat launching. Cabins, two-night minimum, or weekly basis.

Best time to visit: Off-season for hiking, bicycling, wildlife observation. Summer for interpretive programs, camping.

Activities: Hiking, bicycle trails, self-guided trail, boat launching, picnicking all year. Seasonal camping (no hookups), bathhouses, visitors center, interpretive programs, environmental education center, amphitheater, housekeeping cabins, saltwater fishing.

Concessions: Seasonal camp store, snack bar, and bicycle rental.

Pets: Must be on leash.

Other: Cape Henry Lighthouse at nearby Fort Story. Permits for primitive camping at False Cape State Park must be applied for in person here.

For more information:
Seashore State Park and Natural Area, 2500 Shore Drive, Virginia Beach, VA 23451 (804-481-2131 or 804-786-1712). For reservations, call 800-933-7275.

VIRGINIA LIVING MUSEUM

If you're looking for a way to interest your children in natural science, consider the Virginia Living Museum. With its live animal exhibits, indoor and outdoor walk-in aviaries, planetarium, aquarium, and hands-on approach to learning, this is a place that children (and more than a few adults) take to like otters to water.

The private, non-profit corporation that runs the museum puts a premium on accurate and authentic habitats for the native plants and animals on display. In fact, the British Broadcasting Corporation (BBC) selected the museum for a segment of its *Nature* television series depicting America as it was before British colonization.

Bring your camera. Animals such as fox, beaver, bobcat, raccoon, white-tailed deer, and even bald eagles are close to the pathway. Birds and ducks in the glass-enclosed, climate-controlled aviary are accustomed to humans and may ignore your presence altogether. One gregarious and curious flicker actually followed us down the winding staircase.

One unusual feature is a sixty-foot-long tank representing life in Virginia's James River. The tale begins with native trout and crayfish of the cool mountain streams, continues with the famous smallmouth bass of the Piedmont, and ends in a 3,000-gallon ocean tank, complete with sea turtle and sharks.

Where: Newport News. From I-64, take exit 258-A; go south on J. Clyde Morris Boulevard two miles to museum, on left.

Hours: Memorial Day to Labor Day, 9:00 A.M. to 6:00 P.M. Monday to Saturday (until 9:00 P.M. Thursday), 10:00 A.M. to 6:00 P.M. Sunday. Labor Day to Memorial Day, 9:00 A.M. to 5:00 P.M. Monday to Saturday (and 7:00 P.M. to 9:00 P.M. Thursday), 1:00 P.M. to 5:00 P.M. Sunday. Four planetarium shows a day plus one on Thursday evenings, mid-June to Labor Day. Shows at 3:30 P.M. every day, Labor Day to mid-June, plus a Thursday evening show and two additional early afternoon shows on Saturdays and Sundays. Closed New Year's Day, Thanksgiving, Christmas Eve, and Christmas.

Admission: Moderate fee for adults, less for children, fifty cents extra for planetarium. Children under three admitted free; children under four not admitted to planetarium. Small fee for planetarium-only tickets.

Best time to visit: For best animal activity, avoid extremely hot or cold days, or come early on summer mornings. Come anytime for glass-enclosed aviary and other indoor activities. Ask at information desk for schedule of animal feedings. Hours of 1:30 P.M. to 3:30 P.M. Saturdays and Sundays are most crowded.

Activities: Outdoor wild animal exhibits, indoor mountain-to-sea aquarium, touch tank for children, large glass-enclosed indoor aviary and outdoor wetland aviary, planetarium shows, botanical preserve, science museum, on-site and at-school educational programs. Picnic tables on the grounds. Full shelters and grills at nearby Deer Park. Wheelchair access to all attractions, but slightly steep grade on outside path usually requires a helper.

Concessions: Museum store.

Pets: Not allowed.

Other: Nearby Mariner's Museum, with country's most extensive international maritime collection. Fine Arts Center also nearby.

For more information:

Virginia Living Museum, 524 J. Clyde Morris Boulevard, Newport News, VA 23601 (804-595-1900). For information on nearby attractions and hotel reservations, call 800-333-7787.

VIRGINIA MARINE SCIENCE MUSEUM

Have you ever stood face to face wiht a 50-pound red drum fish? Have you ever tonged for oysters just like a Chesapeake Bay waterman? Would you like to know what it's like to go deep under the ocean surface inside a diving machine? Or how about seeing and touching a live horseshoe crab, instead of just wondering about the big empty dark-brown shell you found on a beach?

If you're curious and enjoy science and marine life, and if you have a couple of hours to spare, then the Virginia Marine Science Museum at Virginia Beach was created for you.

The facility is housed in a handsome alabaster-white building about a mile south of the busy Virginia Beach resort strip. Despite the attractiveness of its quarters, we were apprehensive about giving up a beautiful afternoon for a museum. But we were pleasantly surprised. This is no ordinary museum of dusty mounted fish and wall plaques. The Virginia Marine Science Museum incorporates a hands-on approach to exploring marine life and is a place the whole family will enjoy.

The exhibits are interactive. You can sit in a sportfishing chair to feel the tug on the line as you reel in a huge imaginary tarpon. With the push of a button or the pull of a lever, you can create your own wave or learn how to forecast a storm.

On winter weekends and during the summer season, you can watch an artist carve working decoys, learn about the first watermen—the area's Native Americans—and watch a scuba-diving demonstration.

The museum has a 50,000-gallon aquarium that is spellbinding. From a dark passageway, you watch a tremendous variety of saltwater fish, illuminated from above as if in a sunlit ocean. The distinct feeling is that you are with the fish rather than outside looking in. Tautog, red drum, and triggerfish swim by the invisible glass. Snapper, shark, and skate live in apparent harmony. A cobia endlessly rides a ray piggyback, gliding just an inch above the big fish, much the way geese fly in formation to make efficient use of air currents.

Bring binoculars for the outdoor boardwalk excursion into Owls Creek Salt Marsh Preserve, where you might see a yellow-crowned night heron among the reeds or a ruby-throated hummingbird checking out the cardinal flower.

Ever wonder where the expression "thin as a rail" originated? Look for the secretive clapper rail here, compressing its body stalk-thin as it moves among the grasses without touching them.

See that crested duck sitting low in the water? That's a sure sign it's a diving duck. The lack of buoyancy makes it easier to dive for fish in the marsh. This one turns out to be a red-breasted merganser and, sure enough, it disappears beneath the surface as we approach it.

We came away feeling as if we had just skimmed the surface of all there is to see and do. The designers of the Virginia Marine Science Museum have put learning and fun together in a way that creative schoolteachers will welcome.

A $35 million expansion is under way, already adding another 50,000-gallon tank with rays. Plans include a 300,000-gallon and a 75,000-gallon aquarium. Upon completion, the Virginia Marine Science Museum will rank among the top ten aquariums in the country, said a museum spokesperson.

Where: Virginia Beach, General Booth Boulevard, just south of the Rudee Inlet bridge.

Hours: September to mid-June, 9:00 A.M. to 5:00 P.M. daily. June 15 to Labor Day, 9:00 A.M. to 9:00 P.M. Monday to Saturday. 9:00 A.M. to 5:00 P.M. Sunday.

Admission: Fee for adults and children. Group rates available with prior arrangement.

Best time to visit: 11:00 A.M. weekends in off-season and 6:30

P.M. Monday to Saturday summer season for scuba demonstrations; 12:00 P.M. daily year-round for ray feedings; throughout day year-round for other aquarium feedings.

Activities: Indoor scuba demonstration, freshwater and saltwater fish feedings, touch tank, tonging for oysters, diving-capsule simulator, wave-making machine, sportfishing chair, decoy carving demonstration, outdoor salt marsh boardwalk.

Concessions: Gift shop open daily, year-round.

Pets: Not allowed.

Other: Educational programs for schools and community groups.

For more information:

Virginia Marine Science Museum, 717 General Booth Boulevard, Virginia Beach, VA 23451 (804-437-4949).

VIRGINIA ZOOLOGICAL PARK

The antics of the long-armed gibbons—those Tarzan-like acrobats of Southeast Asia treetops—hold visitors spellbound at the Virginia Zoological Park. To some extent, it is the animal's human qualities that rivet the attention. The gibbon is the smallest of the apes and the only primate (besides humans) that walks upright at all times.

Although not a large facility as zoos go, Virginia Zoological Park has some notable features. A magnet for children is the spacious waterfowl pond, which provides a home for a variety of colorful and gregarious ducks—mallards, wood ducks, pochards, and mandarins. Vending bins dispense handfuls of food that youngsters can use to lure the ducks closer.

Also visit the Botanical Conservatory, a turn-of-the-century building exhibiting tropical and desert plants in natural settings.

It's easy to see why sloth is not a desirable state when you watch the languid pace of the two-toed sloth. This animal of tropical jungles conducts life's normal functions—eating, sleeping, mating, and giving birth—while hanging upside-down in trees.

American bison, which once roamed the plains in large numbers similar to the wildebeest in Africa and caribou in Alaska, now wander the zoo grounds at Lafayette Park.

As you walk the grounds, notice the gardens and landscaped animal exhibits. Much of this work is done by the Volunteers of Zoo Horticulture. In fact, the daily operation of the zoo is made possible by various volunteer groups, including Friends of the Zoo, the Docent Council (serving as tour guides), the Tidewater Raptor Society, and Keeper Aides.

The zoo has recently acquired two female Siberian tigers. We were concerned that for many years the large cats have been housed in rather small quarters. A spokesperson said the zoo is in the process of raising money to build a larger African exhibit.

Other exhibits include small mammals, reptiles, birds of prey, marine mammals, large mammals, and hoofed animals.

Where: Lafayette Park, Norfolk. From I-64, take exit 276, go south on US 460 (Granby Street) about three miles to the park, on left.

Hours: 10:00 A.M. to 5:00 P.M. daily, except Christmas and New Year's. Free hour, 4:00 P.M. to 5:00 P.M. Sundays and Mondays.

Admission: Small fee for adults, less for children and senior citizens.

Best time to visit: Elephant demonstrations 2:00 P.M. daily, spring through fall, and 2:00 P.M. Saturdays and Sundays in winter. Avoid temperature extremes to see animals in most active state.

Activities: Outdoor and indoor wild animal exhibits, paved walkways for strollers and wheelchairs, other facilities for disabled. Picnic facilities outside zoo in Lafayette Park. Guided tours by reservation. Animal visits to schools, retirement homes, and other settings.

Concessions: Concession stand, gift shop.

Pets: Not allowed.

Other: Nearby Norfolk Botanical Garden.

For more information:

Virginia Zoological Park, 3500 Granby Street, Norfolk, VA 23504 (804-441-5227).

WESTMORELAND STATE PARK

Flowing by the spreading green fields and cool oak-hickory forests of Westmoreland State Park is the historic Potomac River. The river has widened and calmed by the time it reaches Westmoreland Park and Chesapeake Bay, after a turbulent trip over Great Falls above Washington, D.C.

Saltwater fishing is excellent on the river. Anglers will find that the park area meets all their needs — marinas, a launch ramp for powerboats, a restaurant overlooking the river, campgrounds, cabins, and showers.

Westmoreland is a place to go fishing and take the family. Water activities in general are a big attraction in the heat of summer, and swimmers may choose between an Olympic-sized pool or the river. Paddleboats and rowboats may be rented.

At the visitors center, park staff will tell you where to look for fossil remains of ancient marine animals buried in sediment. They can also provide you with a brochure for the self-guiding Big Meadows Interpretive Trail, with its history of the Powhatan tribe.

If you see a huge bird with a wide wingspan and white head, it may be a bald eagle. They're making a comeback on the Potomac after a serious decline in population for many years.

Nearby Caledon Natural Area serves as a summer home to these impressive birds.

The Northern Neck of Virginia, the peninsula where Westmoreland is located, has several other attractions. Nearby is Wakefield—George Washington's birthplace—and Stratford Hall—General Robert E. Lee's birthplace. Both are open to the public on a seasonal basis.

You can also buy fresh seafood, shop for antiques and crafts, pick your own berries at local berry farms, and sample Virginia wines from a winery.

Where: From Fredericksburg, take State 3 east about forty-three miles, then go north on State 347 a short distance to park entrance.

Hours: Hiking trails and boat launch 8:00 A.M. until dark, year-round. Campgrounds and housekeeping cabins open in spring, close in fall. Pool and interpretive programs, Memorial Day weekend to Labor Day.

Admission: Small parking fee. Swimming, camping, cabin rental, boat-launching fees.

Best time to visit: Summer for beachfront activities, interpretive programs, pool. Anytime for hiking. Spring through fall for picnicking, fishing, crabbing.

Activities: Swimming, boating, camping (hookups available), group camping, saltwater fishing and crabbing, boat launching (motorboats permitted), picnicking, hiking, self-guiding trail, bridle trails, amphitheater, interpretive programs, visitors center.

Concessions: Camp store, restaurant, rowboat and paddleboat rental, long-term and overnight cabins.

Pets: Must be on leash.

For more information:

Westmoreland State Park, Route 1, Box 600, Montross, VA 22520 (804-493-8821 or 804-786-1712).

YORK RIVER STATE PARK

For a change of pace, would you be interested in the fossilized remains of a whale tooth millions of years old in the soft soil of the York River?

Or maybe digging your fingers into muck that was once an ancient sea, and touching the bumpy surface of a porpoise vertebra?

York River State Park, located near Williamsburg, has an unusual attraction—fossil hunting. In fact, the park's Croaker Landing is an archaeological site on the National Register of Historic Places.

In addition to the remains of such vertebrates as whale, porpoise, shark, and fish, you can unearth prehistoric shells of gastropods, pelecypods, and coelenterates. No, they're not dinosaurs; they're invertebrates such as snails, oysters, clams, corals, and anemones. Fossils found on river and stream banks at the park were left from an ocean that long ago covered Tidewater Virginia all the way to Richmond.

One of the park's hiking trails, the Mattaponi (pronounced mat-a-pone-EYE), takes you to a beach area where cliffs have eroded, exposing the fossils. You might also find fossils along feeder streams, especially after a heavy rain has caused bank erosion.

Fossil remains are just part of the story at York River State Park. This coastal estuary, where the river's freshwater and saltwater meet, is also noted for its rich variety of present-day marine plants and animals. The sprawling and delicately balanced Chesapeake Bay—locked in a critical battle with overdevelopment, pollution, and overharvesting—relies heavily for its sustenance on such nursery areas in feeder rivers such as the York. The abundance of life in the marshes and river here is tribute to the park's fundamental purpose—that of protecting a finely

A great horned owl

balanced ecosystem while at the same time providing access for people to enjoy it. In fact, York River served as a model in developing resource management plans for Virginia's other state parks.

There are more than fifteen miles of hiking, bicycling, and bridle trails at this park. Or you may prefer canoe touring, a popular way to savor the natural areas of the salt marsh here. Every weekend, spring through fall, park interpreters guide canoeists along the Taskinas Creek wetlands, where red-winged blackbirds call from the reeds, and long-legged wading birds poise motionless above their prey in shallow water. You'll see why the watershed surrounding this creek is a Chesapeake Bay National Estuarine Research Reserve, a designation that gives it added protection and offers valuable opportunities for research. Be sure to reserve your canoe with a phone call before your arrival.

Many anglers fish for bluegill and largemouth bass in the freshwater of Woodstock Pond. Others prefer launching a boat at Croaker Landing in the brackish water of the York River to try for the plentiful croaker, trout, spot, catfish, and crabs. Construction of a fishing pier is in the plans for this park.

Where: James City County, one mile northeast of I-64 (exit 231) and eleven miles northwest of Williamsburg.

Hours: 8:00 A.M. until dusk, year-round, except for two-week closing in early to mid-November for controlled deer hunt. Canoe tours spring through fall weekends, 8:30 A.M. to 10:30 A.M. Saturdays and 4:00 P.M. to 6:00 P.M. Sundays, by reservation.

Admission: Small parking fee. Fee for canoe tours and boat launching.

Best time to visit: Anytime for trail use, spring and fall weekends for canoe tours, Memorial Day to Labor Day for interpretive programs.

Activities: Guided canoe tours, guided hikes, visitors center, boat launch and dock (motorboats permitted), bicycling and horseback riding, wildlife observation, observation tower, seine netting, picnic shelters overlooking York River (may be reserved), saltwater and freshwater fishing, environmental education including studies of fossils, marine life, wetlands.

Concessions: Vending machines.

Pets: Must be on leash.

Other: Estuaries Day, the third Saturday of September.

For more information:

York River State Park, 5526 Riverview Road, Williamsburg, VA 23188 (804-566-3036 or 804-786-1712).

4

Canoe Trails

Whether cruising for a week or a weekend, canoeists who love the slap of riffles against a canoe bottom can find everything from placid currents to raging whitewater in Virginia.

In Tidewater and coastal Virginia, the water is flat. Wind and mosquitoes may be your biggest challenges.

But rivers cascading out of Virginia's mountains—the James, the New, the Maury, and the Russell, for instance—alternate between flat water and exciting rapids. Certain sections offer the adventurous about as much excitement as they can handle.

The James River builds to dangerous class 5 rapids in downtown Richmond, for example, during high-water periods. Canoe water is rated from class 1 to class 6. The best way to describe class 6 rapids is to say that people with death wishes love them. The movie *Deliverance* had class 5 to 6 water. The city of Richmond requires a $10.00 permit from users of the river during high water. Someone needs to know you're out there, because you may well need to be rescued.

Canoeists on unfamiliar water need detailed instructions.

We recommend two guidebooks—one for inland rivers (mostly freshwater) and the second for rivers and coves around Chesapeake Bay.

The first is *Classic Virginia Rivers—A Paddler's Guide to Premier Whitewater and Scenic Float Trips in the Old Dominion*, by Ed Grove. The author has compiled essential canoeing information on more than eighty Virginia rivers and crammed it into this 352-page book.

At-a-glance data sheets provide an instant overview of each river—the difficulty, floatable water levels, what scenery and wildlife to look for, where you might have to portage, where to put in and take out, even water velocity and gradient (two pieces of essential information that determine whether you'll be riding a monster or an easy chair). To order, send $18.00 postpaid to Ed Grove, 2420 North George Mason Drive, Arlington, VA 22207-1755, or call 703-533-8334.

The book on saltwater and tidal rivers is *Exploring the Chesapeake in Small Boats* by John Page Williams Jr. Williams tells how to choose a canoe, what insect repellent to use, where to put in and take out around the bay, and how to soak up the bay's ecology, geology, and human history. The book is available from bookstores around the bay, or from Tidewater Publishers, Centreville, MD 21617 (800-638-7641).

Finally, the state provides a fact sheet with brief river descriptions, information resources, canoeing clubs in Virginia, and other helpful tips. Contact the Department of Conservation and Recreation, 203 Governor Street, Suite 302, Richmond, VA 23219 (804-786-1712).

Here are some of the canoe dealers and rental liveries that we've found helpful around the state:

James River

James River Basin Canoe Livery, Route 4, Box 125, Lexington, VA 24450 (703-261-7334).

James River Reeling and Rafting, P.O. Box 757, Scottsville, VA 24590 (804-286-4386).

James River Runners, Route 4, Box 106, Scottsville, VA 24590 (804-286-2338).

West View Livery & Outfitters, 1151 West View Road, P.O. Box 258, Goochland, VA 23063 (804-457-2744).

Shenandoah River

Shenandoah River Outfitters, Route 3, Luray, VA 22835 (703-743-4159).

Downriver Canoe Company, Route 1, Box 256-A, Bentonville, VA 22610 (703-635-5526).

River Rental Outfitters, P.O. Box 145, Bentonville, VA 22610 (703-635-5050).

Front Royal Canoe Company, P.O. Box 473, Front Royal, VA 22630 (703-635-5440).

Rappahannock and Rapidan Rivers

Rappahannock River Campground, 33017 River Mill Road, Richardsville, VA 22736 (703-399-1839).

Appomattox River

Appomattox River Company, Farmville, VA 23901 (804-392-6645).

For a free "Appomattox River Canoe Guide," showing maps and launch sites, contact County of Chesterfield, Parks and Recreation, P.O. Box 40, Chesterfield, VA 23832 (804-748-1623).

RIVER OTTER

The mammal with the bewhiskered and worldly-wise face of the old gent on the National Bohemian bottle is the playful prankster of the river world, one of the few animals that appear to take unending delight in the sheer joy of living.

River otters are fun to watch. They love play for play's sake, rollicking in the water and endlessly sliding down mudbanks or snowbanks into a river or pond. Their diet consists mainly of crayfish and other crustaceans, as well as amphibians and fish.

Canoeists and anglers east of the mountains in Virginia occasionally see the bright eyes and gleaming shiny head of an otter in the flat, slow-moving rivers of Piedmont and Tidewater Virginia.

Historically, the river otter was one of the most widespread mammals west of the Blue Ridge, too, say biologists. But intensive hunting, trapping, and farming took their toll on the otter, as well as on the buffalo, mountain lion, elk, and wolf. Efforts are under way to restock the otter in western Virginia rivers. Look for them especially on the Cowpasture River between Clifton Forge and Williamsville in Bath County.

Index

APPALACHIAN TRAIL
General information, 1–3
George Washington National
Forest, 34
Grayson Highlands State
Park, 41–45
James River Face and
Thunder Ridge
Wilderness Areas, 55
Jefferson National Forest, 52
Mount Rogers National
Recreation Area, 62–66
Mountain Lake Wilderness
Area, 56–57
Shenandoah National Park,
3–12
Sky Meadows State Park,
74–78
White Rocks Campground,
58
AQUARIUMS
Virginia Living Museum,
161–162
Virginia Marine Science
Museum, 163–165
ARTS AND CRAFTS
Breaks Interstate Park, 15–19
Chippokes Plantation State
Park, 128–129
Claytor Lake State Park,
20–22
Cumberland Gap National
Historical Park, 22–25

Hungry Mother State Park,
45–47

BERRY-PICKING and
HERBING
Clinch Mountain Wildlife
Management Area, 54
BICYCLING. *See also*
MOUNTAIN BIKING
Back Bay National Wildlife
Refuge, 107–112
Blue Ridge Parkway, 3–12
Chincoteague National
Wildlife Refuge,
122–127
Chippokes Plantation State
Park, 128–129
Fairy Stone State Park,
27–30
False Cape State Park,
107–112
Kiptopeke State Park,
134–138
Lake Drummond, 130–131
Meadowlark Gardens
Regional Park, 157–158
Mount Rogers National
Recreation Area, 62–66
New River Trail State Park,
69–72
Pocahontas State Park,
102–106

Seashore State Park and
    Natural Area, 158–161
Shenandoah National Park,
    3–12
Skyline Drive, 3–12
Twin Lakes State Park,
    95–98
Virginia Creeper Trail, 80–82
Washington and Old
    Dominion Railroad
    Regional Park, 151–153
York River State Park,
    169–171
BIRD-WATCHING
Back Bay National Wildlife
    Refuge, 107–112
banding project, Kiptopeke
    State Park, 134–138
Bethel Beach Natural Area
    Preserve, 121–122
Bull Run Regional Park,
    153–156
Caledon Natural Area,
    112–114
Chesapeake Bay, 115–122
Chincoteague National
    Wildlife Refuge, 122–127
Clinch Mountain Wildlife
    Management Area, 54
Daingerfield Island, 146
Dyke Marsh, 146
Eastern Shore Birding
    Festival, Kiptopeke State
    Park, 134–138
False Cape State Park,
    107–112
Fort Hunt Park, 145
Great Dismal Swamp,
    129–134

Hawk-watching, 10
James River Park, 89–92
Jefferson National Forest,
    47–58
Kiptopeke State Park,
    134–138
Lake Anna State Park, 92–95
Lake Drummond, 130–131
Leesylvania State Park,
    138–140
Loon, The, 85
Meadowlark Gardens
    Regional Park, 157–158
Mount Vernon Trail, 143–147
Norfolk Botanical Garden,
    147–149
Pohick Bay Regional Park,
    141–143
Sky Meadows State Park,
    74–78
Virginia Living Museum,
    161–162
Virginia Marine Science
    Museum, 163–164
BOATING
Bark Camp Lake, 53
Bear Creek Lake State Park,
    96–98
Breaks Interstate Park, 15–19
Buggs Island Lake and Lake
    Gaston, 83–89
Bull Run Marina, 155–156
Douthat State Park, 25–27
Dyke Marsh, 146
Fairy Stone State Park, 27–30
False Cape State Park,
    107–112
Fountainhead Regional Park,
    155–156

Great Dismal Swamp,
    129–134
Holliday Lake State Park,
    96–98
Hungry Mother State Park,
    45–47
James River Park, 89–92
Lake Keokee, 56
Lake Anna State Park, 92–95
Lake Moomaw, 58–62
Leesylvania State Park,
    138–140
Mason Neck State Park,
    140–143
Occoneechee State Park.
    84–87
Occoquan, 154
Philpott Reservoir, 29
Pocahontas State Park,
    102–106
Pohick Bay Regional Park,
    141–143
Sandy Run (rowing), 154
Seashore State Park and
    Natural Area, 158–161
Sherando Lake, 41
Smith Mountain Lake State
    Park, 78–80
Staunton River State Park,
    84–87
Twin Lakes State Park, 95–98
Westmoreland State Park,
    167–168
York River State Park,
    169–171
BOTANICAL GARDENS
Botanical Conservatory,
    Virginia Zoological
    Park, 165–167

Chippokes Plantation State
    Park, 128–129
Gunston Hall, 141–143
Lewis Ginter Botanical
    Garden, 98–100
Maymont, 100–102
Meadowlark Gardens
    Regional Park, 157–158
Norfolk Botanical Garden,
    147–149
River Farm, 145

CAMPING. *See also*
    PRIMITIVE CAMPING
Bark Camp Lake, 53
Bear Creek Lake State Park,
    96–98
Blue Ridge Parkway, 3–12
Breaks Interstate Park, 15–19
Buggs Island Lake and Lake
    Gaston, 83–89
Bull Run Regional Park,
    153–156
Cave Springs Recreation
    Area, 56
Chincoteague National
    Wildlife Refuge,
    122–127
Chippokes Plantation State
    Park, 128–129
Cumberland Gap National
    Historical Park, 22–25
Douthat State Park, 25–27
Fairy Stone State Park,
    27–30
False Cape State Park,
    107–112
Fenwick Mines Wetlands, 53

George Washington National
      Forest, 30–41
Grayson Highlands State
      Park, 41–45
Hidden Valley, 36–37
High Knob, 54–55
Holliday Lake State Park,
      96–98
Hungry Mother State Park,
      45–47
James River Face and
      Thunder Ridge
      Wilderness Areas, 55
Jefferson National Forest,
      47–58
Kiptopeke State Park,
      134–138
Lake Anna State Park, 92–95
Lake Moomaw, 58–62
Massanutten Mountain and
      Fort Valley, 39
Mount Rogers National
      Recreation Area, 62–66
Natural Tunnel State Park,
      66–69
Occoneechee State Park.
      84–87
Philpott Reservoir, 29
Pocahontas State Park,
      102–106
Pohick Bay Regional Park,
      141–143
Prince William Forest Park,
      139–140
Seashore State Park and
      Natural Area, 158–161
Seven Sisters Trail, 58
Shawvers Run Wilderness
      Area, 58

Sherando Lake, 41
Skyline Drive, 3–12
Smith Mountain Lake State
      Park, 78–80
Staunton River State Park,
      84–87
Todd Lake, 41
Twin Lakes State Park, 95–98
Westmoreland State Park,
      167–168
White Rocks Campground,
      58
CANOEING and KAYAKING
Breaks Interstate Park, 15–19
Bull Run Marina, 155–156
Chincoteague National
      Wildlife Refuge, 122–127
Clinch Mountain Wildlife
      Management Area, 54
dealers, liveries, 172–174
False Cape State Park,
      107–112
George Washington National
      Forest, 30–41
guidebooks, fact sheet, 173
Hungry Mother State Park,
      45–47
James River Park, 89–92
Leesylvania State Park,
      138–140
New River Trail State Park,
      69–72
Staunton River State Park,
      84–87
York River State Park,
      169–171
CRABBING
Chincoteague National
      Wildlife Refuge, 122–127

Westmoreland State Park,
167–168
CROSS-COUNTRY SKIING
Blue Ridge Parkway, 3–12
Hungry Mother State Park,
45–47
Mount Rogers National
Recreation Area,
62–66
Pocahontas State Park,
102–106
Shenandoah National Park,
3–12
Skyline Drive, 3–12
CRUISES
Chesapeake Bay, 115–122
Claytor Lake State Park,
20–22
Tangier Island, 120–121

DRIVES
Blue Ridge Parkway, 3–12
Cumberland Gap National
Historical Park, 22–25
Highland Scenic Tour, 37–38
Mount Rogers National
Recreation Area, 62–66
Mount Vernon Trail,
143–147
Shenandoah National Park,
3–12
Skyline Drive, 3–12

FAMILY RECREATION
Breaks Interstate Park, 15–19
Bull Run Regional Park,
153–156

children's garden, Lewis
Ginter Botanical Garden,
98–100
Chippokes Plantation State
Park, 128–129
Claytor Lake State Park,
20–22
Fenwick Mines Wetlands, 53
Fountainhead Regional Park,
155–156
Mount Rogers National
Recreation Area, 62–66
petting farm, Maymont,
100–102
Pocahontas State Park,
102–106
River Farm, 145
Staunton River State Park,
84–87
Virginia Living Museum,
161–162
FISHING. *See also* CRABBING
Amelia Wildlife Management
Area, 97
Back Bay National Wildlife
Refuge, 110
Bark Camp Lake, 53
Bear Creek Lake State Park,
96–98
Breaks Interstate Park,
15–19
Buggs Island Lake (Kerr
Reservoir), 83–84
Bull Run Marina, 155–156
Chesapeake Bay
Bridge.Tunnel, 118–119
Chesapeake Bay, 115–122
Chippokes Plantation State
Park, 128–129

Claytor Lake State Park,
  20–22
Clinch Mountain Wildlife
  Management Area, 54
Douthat State Park, 25–27
Elkhorn Lake, 41
Fairy Stone State Park,
  27–30
Fountainhead Regional Park,
  155–156
George Washington National
  Forest, 30–41
Goshen Pass, 36
Grayson Highlands State
  Park, 41–45
Great Falls Park, 146–147
Hidden Valley, 36–37
High Knob, 54–55
Holliday Lake State Park,
  96–98
Hungry Mother State Park,
  45–47
James River Park, 89–92
Jefferson National Forest,
  47–58
Jones Point Lighthouse, 146
Kiptopeke State Park,
  134–138
Lake Drummond, 130–131
Lake Gaston, 83–84
Lake Moomaw, 58–62
Lake Keokee, 56
Lake Anna State Park, 92–95
Leesylvania State Park,
  138–140
Mason Neck State Park,
  140–143
Mount Rogers National
  Recreation Area, 62–66

New River Trail State Park,
  69–72
Occoneechee State Park.
  84–87
Occoquan, 154
Philpott Reservoir, 29
Pocahontas State Park,
  102–106
Pohick Bay Regional Park,
  141–143
Ramsey's Draft Wilderness
  Area, 40
Seven Sisters Trail, 58
Shawvers Run Wilderness
  Area, 58
Sherando Lake, 41
Sky Meadows State Park,
  74–78
Sky Meadows State Park,
  74–78
Smith Mountain Lake State
  Park, 78–80
Staunton River State Park,
  84–87
tournaments, Smith Mountain
  Lake State Park, 78–80
Twin Lakes State Park,
  95–98
Westmoreland State Park,
  167–168
White Rocks Campground,
  58
York River State Park,
  169–171

GEOLOGICAL
  ATTRACTIONS
caverns, 19–20, 57

Fairy Stone State Park, 27–30
Natural Bridge, 57
Natural Chimneys, 41
Natural Tunnel, 66–69
New River Trail State Park,
    69–72
Twin Pinnacles, Grayson
    Highlands State Park,
    41–45
GOLF
Pohick Bay Regional Park,
    141–143

HANDICAPPED ACCESS
Douthat State Park, 25–27
frangrance garden for blind,
    Norfolk Botanical
    Garden, 147–149
ramp to ocean, Chincoteague
    National Wildlife Refuge,
    122–127
trail for blind, Massanutten
    Mountain and Fort
    Valley, 39
Virginia Zoological Park,
    165–167
wheelchair trail, Pocahontas
    State Park, 102–106
HIKING. *See also* NATURE
    WALKS
Appalachian Trail, 1–3
Bark Camp Lake, 53
Bear Creek Lake State Park,
    96–98
Blue Ridge Parkway, 3–12
Breaks Interstate Park, 15–19
Caledon Natural Area,
    112–114

Cascades National Recreation
    Trail, 53–54
Chincoteague National
    Wildlife Refuge,
    122–127
Chippokes Plantation State
    Park, 128–129
Claytor Lake State Park,
    20–22
Cumberland Gap National
    Historical Park, 22–25
Daingerfield Island, 146
Douthat State Park, 25–27
Fairy Stone State Park,
    27–30
False Cape State Park,
    107–112
Fenwick Mines Wetlands, 53
Fort Hunt Park, 145
Fountainhead Regional Park,
    155–156
George Washington National
    Forest, 30–41
Grayson Highlands State
    Park, 41–45
Great Falls Park, 146–147
Hemlock Overlook Regional
    Park, 154–156
Hidden Valley, 36–37
High Knob, 54–55
Hungry Mother State Park,
    45–47
James River Park, 89–92
James River Face and
    Thunder Ridge
    Wilderness Areas, 55
Jefferson National Forest,
    47–58
Lake Anna State Park, 92–95

Lake Moomaw, 58–62
Lake Drummond, 130–131
Leesylvania State Park,
    138–140
Longdale Recreation Area, 38
Mason Neck Wildlife
    Refuge, 141–143
Mason Neck State Park,
    140–143
Meadowlark Gardens
    Regional Park, 157–158
Mount Rogers National
    Recreation Area, 62–66
Natural Tunnel State Park,
    66–69
New River Trail State Park,
    69–72
North Mountain Trail, 39–40
Occoneechee State Park.
    84–87
Pocahontas State Park,
    102–106
Prince William Forest Park,
    139–140
Ramsey's Draft Wilderness
    Area, 40
Red Rock Wilderness
    Overlook Regional Park,
    156–157
Roaring Run National
    Recreation Trail, 57
Seashore State Park and
    Natural Area, 158–161
Seven Sisters Trail, 58
Shenandoah National Park,
    3–12
Skyline Drive, 3–12
Smith Mountain Lake State
    Park, 78–80

St. Mary's Wilderness Area,
    40–41
Staunton River State Park,
    84–87
Todd Lake, 41
Virginia Creeper Trail,
    80–82
Westmoreland State Park,
    167–168
Wild Oak National
    Recreation Trail, 41
York River State Park,
    169–171
HORSEBACK RIDING
    Breaks Interstate Park, 15–19
    Bull Run Regional Park,
        153–156
    Clinch Mountain Wildlife
        Management Area, 54
    Grayson Highlands State
        Park, 41–45
    Hungry Mother State Park,
        45–47
    Meadowlark Gardens
        Regional Park, 157–158
    Mount Rogers National
        Recreation Area, 62–66
    New River Trail State Park,
        69–72
    Pohick Bay Regional Park,
        141–143
    Virginia Creeper Trail, 80–82
    Washington and Old
        Dominion Railroad
        Regional Park, 151–153
    Westmoreland State Park,
        167–168
    York River State Park,
        169–171

HORSE CAMPING
Barbours Creek Wilderness,
52,53
Grayson Highlands State
Park, 41–45
Jefferson National Forest,
47–58
Mount Rogers National
Recreation Area, 62–66
Sky Meadows State Park,
74–78
HUNTING
Amelia Wildlife Management
Area, 97
Bear Creek Lake State Park,
96–98
Breaks Interstate Park, 15–19
Grayson Highlands State
Park, 41–45
Jefferson National Forest,
47–58
Occoneechee State Park.
84–87
Pocahontas State Park,
102–106
Sherando Lake, 41
Sky Meadows State Park,
74–78

ICE SKATING
Hungry Mother State Park,
45–47
Virginia Creeper Trail, 80–82

LEARNING ACTIVITIES
Back Bay National Wildlife
Refuge, 110

Caledon Natural Area,
112–114
curriculum guide, xii
Douthat State Park, 25–27
False Cape State Park,
107–112
Hemlock Overlook Regional
Park, 154–155
Holliday Lake State Park,
96–98
Lake Anna State Park,
92–95
Lewis Ginter Botanical
Garden, 98–100
Mason Neck State Park,
140–142
Mason Neck Wildlife
Refuge, 141–143
Norfolk Botanical Garden,
147–149
Pochahontas State Park,
102–106
Seashore State Park and
Natural Area, 158–161
Sky Meadows State Park,
74–78
Virginia Zoological Park,
165–167
Virginia Living Museum,
161–162
Virginia Marine Science
Museum, 163–164
York River State Park,
169–171
LODGING
Blue Ridge Parkway, 3–12
Breaks Interstate Park, 15–19
Cedar Crest Conference
Center, 96

Chippokes Plantation State Park, 128–129

Claytor Lake State Park, 20–22

Douthat State Park, 25–27

Fairy Stone State Park, 27–30

Mountain Lake Wilderness Area, 56–57

Pocahontas State Park, 102–106

Seashore State Park and Natural Area, 158–161

Skyline Drive, 3–12

Smith Mountain Lake State Park, 78–80

Staunton River State Park, 84–87

Twin Lakes State Park, 95–98

Wintergreen Resort, 12–14

MOUNTAIN BIKING. *See also* BICYCLING

George Washington National Forest, 30–41

Seven Sisters Trail, 58

MUSEUMS, EXHIBITS, and HISTORIC HOMES

antebellum farmhouse, Sky Meadows State Park, 74–78

Appomattox Courthouse, Appomattox National Historical Park, 97

Bloemendaal House, Lewis Ginter Botanical Garden, 99

Civil War encampments, Sky Meadows State Park, 78

Coal Museum, Natural Tunnel State Park, 67

Dooley mansion, Maymont, 100

Farm and Forestry Museum, Chippokes Plantation State Park, 128–129

farmsteads, Cumberland Gap National Historical Park, 23

frontier town, Virginia Creeper Trail, 81

Gunston Hall Plantation, 141–143

homestead, Grayson Highlands State Park, 41–45

Mansion, Chippokes Plantation State Park, 128–129

mining exhibit, Lake Anna State Park, 94

Mountain farm, Blue Ridge Parkway, 5

Museum of American Frontier Culture, 12

NASA visitors center, Chincoteague National Wildlife Refuge, 126–127

Prestwould Plantation, Occoneechee State Park. 84–85

Smoot House, Caledon Natural Area, 114

Virginia Marine Science Museum, 163–164

Warwick Mansion, Hidden
     Valley, 36–37
MUSIC
  Bluegrass Festival, Fairy
     Stone State Park, 27–30
  Cumberland Gap National
     Historical Park, 22–25
  Gospel sings, Breaks
     Interstate Park, 15–19

NATURE WALKS. *See also*
  HIKING
  Back Bay National Wildlife
     Refuge, 107–112
  Bull Run Regional Park,
     153–156
  Chessie Nature Trail, 35
  Chincoteague National
     Wildlife Refuge, 122–127
  Chippokes Plantation State
     Park, 128–129
  Claytor Lake State Park,
     20–22
  Cumberland Gap National
     Historical Park, 22–25
  Douthat State Park, 25–27
  Dyke Marsh, 146
  False Cape State Park,
     107–112
  Fenwick Mines Wetlands, 53
  Gunston Hall, 141–143
  Henry Lanum Jr. Trail, 36
  Holliday Lake State Park,
     96–98
  Kiptopeke State Park,
     134–138
  Lake Anna State Park, 92–95
  Lake Drummond, 130–131

Lake Keokee, 56
Leesylvania State Park,
     138–140
Lewis Ginter Botanical
     Garden, 98–100
Mason Neck State Park,
     140–143
Massanutten Mountain and
     Fort Valley, 39
Maymont, 100–102
Meadowlark Gardens
     Regional Park, 157–158
Mount Rogers National
     Recreation Area, 62–66
Mount Vernon Trail, 143–147
New River Trail State Park,
     69–72
Norfolk Botanical Garden,
     147–149
Pocahontas State Park,
     102–106
Pohick Bay Regional Park,
     141–143
River Farm, 145
Seashore State Park and
     Natural Area, 158–161
Sky Meadows State Park,
     74–78
Staunton River State Park,
     84–87
Tangier Island, 120–121
Theodore Roosevelt Island,
     146
Virginia Zoological Park,
     165–167
Virginia Creeper Trail,
     80–82
Virginia Marine Science
     Museum, 163–164

Washington and Old
    Dominion Railroad
    Regional Park, 151–153
Westmoreland State Park,
    167–168
Wintergreen Resort, 12–14

PANNING FOR GOLD
Lake Anna State Park, 92–95
PHOTOGRAPHY
Chincoteague National
    Wildlife Refuge, 122–127
Grayson Highlands State
    Park, 41–45
Great Dismal Swamp,
    129–134
Mason Neck Wildlife
    Refuge, 141–143
Virginia Living Museum,
    161–162
Wintergreen Resort, 12–14
PICNICKING
Bark Camp Lake, 53
Blue Ridge Parkway, 3–12
Breaks Interstate Park, 15–19
Buggs Island Lake and Lake
    Gaston, 83–89
Bull Run Marina, 155–156
Bull Run Regional Park,
    153–156
Caledon Natural Area,
    112–114
Cascades National Recreation
    Trail, 53–54
Chippokes Plantation State
    Park, 128–129
Claytor Lake State Park,
    20–22

Cumberland Gap National
    Historical Park, 22–25
Daingerfield Island, 146
Douthat State Park, 25–27
Dyke Marsh, 146
Fairy Stone State Park,
    27–30
Fenwick Mines Wetlands, 53
Fort Hunt Park, 145
Fountainhead Regional Park,
    155–156
Goshen Pass, 36
Grayson Highlands State
    Park, 41–45
Great Falls Park, 146–147
Gunston Hall, 141–143
High Knob, 54–55
Hungry Mother State Park,
    45–47
James River Face and
    Thunder Ridge
    Wilderness Areas, 55
Jefferson National Forest,
    47–58
Jones Point Lighthouse, 146
Kiptopeke State Park,
    134–138
Lafayette Park, 167
Lake Anna State Park, 92–95
Lake Keokee, 56
Lake Moomaw, 58–62
Leesylvania State Park,
    138–140
Little Stony National
    Recreation Trail, 56
Longdale Recreation Area,
    38
Mason Neck State Park,
    140–143

Maymont, 100–102
Natural Tunnel State Park,
    66–69
New River Trail State Park,
    69–72
Norfolk Botanical Garden,
    147–149
Occoneechee State Park.
    84–87
Pohick Bay Regional Park,
    141–143
Roaring Run National
    Recreation Trail, 57
Seashore State Park and
    Natural Area, 158–161
Seven Sisters Trail, 58
Sherando Lake, 41
Sky Meadows State Park,
    74–78
Skyline Drive, 3–12
Smith Mountain Lake State
    Park, 78–80
Staunton River State Park,
    84–87
Virginia Living Museum,
    161–162
Westmoreland State Park,
    167–168
York River State Park,
    169–171
PRIMITIVE CAMPING
Appalachian Trail, 1–3
Chincoteague National
    Wildlife Refuge,
    122–127
Clinch Mountain Wildlife
    Management Area, 54
Cumberland Gap National
    Historical Park, 22–25

False Cape State Park,
    107–112
George Washington National
    Forest, 30–41
Great Dismal Swamp,
    129–134
Lake Moomaw, 58–62
Mount Rogers National
    Recreation Area, 62–66
Sky Meadows State Park,
    74–78
Smith Mountain Lake State
    Park, 78–80
Virginia Creeper Trail,
    80–82

SHOOTING
Amelia Wildlife Management
    Area, 97
Bull Run Regional Park,
    153–156
SNORKELING
James River Park, 89–92
STARGAZING
Caledon Natural Area,
    112–114
Jefferson National Forest,
    47–58
Virginia Living Museum,
    161–162
SWIMMING
Breaks Interstate Park, 15–19
Buggs Island Lake and Lake
    Gaston, 83–89
Bull Run Regional Park,
    153–156
Cave Springs Recreation
    Area, 56

Chippokes Plantation State Park, 128–129
Claytor Lake State Park, 20–22
Douthat State Park, 25–27
Fairy Stone State Park, 27–30
High Knob, 54–55
Hungry Mother State Park, 45–47
Kiptopeke State Park, 134–138
Lake Anna State Park, 92–95
Lake Moomaw, 58–62
Longdale Recreation Area, 38
Natural Tunnel State Park, 66–69
New River Trail State Park, 69–72
Philpott Reservoir, 29
Pocahontas State Park, 102–106
Pohick Bay Regional Park, 141–143
Smith Mountain Lake State Park, 78–80
Staunton River State Park, 84–87
Todd Lake, 41
Twin Lakes State Park, 95–98
Westmoreland State Park, 167–168

TENNIS
Staunton River State Park, 84–87

TOURS
chairlift, Natural Tunnel State Park, 66–69
mule-drawn wagons, Mount Rogers National Recreation Area, 62–66
Norfolk Botanical Garden, 147–149
Smith Mountain Lake State Park, 78–80
TREES
Beartown Wilderness Area, 53
Clinch Mountain Wildlife Management Area, 54
Cypress Swamp, 159
George Washington National Forest, 30–41
Grayson Highlands State Park, 41–45
Henry Lanum Jr. Trail, 36
Highland Scenic Tour, 37–38
Jefferson National Forest, 47–58
Lake Keokee, 56
Laurel Fork, 38–39
Mount Rogers National Recreation Area, 62–66
Ramsey's Draft Wilderness Area, 40
Smith Mountain Lake State Park, 78–80
TUBING
George Washington National Forest, 30–41
Goshen Pass, 36
James River Park, 89–92

WATERFALLS
Appalachian Trail, 9
Crabtree Falls, 3
Great Falls Park, 146–147
James River Face and
Thunder Ridge
Wilderness Areas, 55
Lake Keokee, 56
Little Stony National
Recreation Trail, 56
St. Mary's Wilderness Area,
40–41
Wintergreen Resort, 12–14
WATERSKIING
Lake Anna State Park, 92–95
Smith Mountain Lake State
Park, 78–80
WILDFLOWERS
Breaks Interstate Park, 15–19
Bull Run Regional Park,
153–156
Fairy Stone State Park, 27–30
G. Richard Thompson
Wildlife Management
Area, 77
Henry Lanum Jr. Trail, 36
Hungry Mother State Park,
45–47
Lake Drummond, 130–131
Natural Tunnel State Park,
66–69
New River Trail State Park,
69–72
Sky Meadows State Park,
74–78
Wintergreen Resort, 12–14
WILDLIFE
Amelia Wildlife Management
Area, 97

animal sign, 50–51
Appalachian Trail, 1–3
Back Bay National Wildlife
Refuge, 107–112
Blue Ridge Parkway, 3–12
Bull Run Regional Park,
153–156
Chincoteague National
Wildlife Refuge,
122–127
Clinch Mountain Wildlife
Management Area, 54
Fairy Stone Wildlife
Management Area, 29
False Cape State Park,
107–112
G. Richard Thompson
Wildlife Management
Area, 77
Grayson Highlands State
Park, 41–45
James River Park, 89–92
Jefferson National Forest,
47–58
Kiptopeke State Park,
134–138
Lake Drummond, 130–131
Lake Keokee, 56
Lake Moomaw, 58–62
Laurel Fork, 38–39
Leesylvania State Park,
138–140
Mason Neck Wildlife
Refuge, 141–143
Maymont, 100–102
Meadowlark Gardens
Regional Park, 157–158
Mount Rogers National
Recreation Area, 62–66

New River Trail State Park,
69–72
Occoneechee State Park.
84–87
Pocahontas State Park,
102–106
Pohick Bay Regional Park,
141–143
Shenandoah National Park,
3–12
Skyline Drive, 3–12
Virginia Creeper Trail, 80–82
Virginia Living Museum,
161–162
Virginia Zoological Park,
165–167
York River State Park,
169–171
Specific animals
Bears
Clinch Mountain Wildlife
Management Area, 54
Shenandoah National Park,
33
Beaver
Lake Anna State Park,
92–95
Laurel Fork, 38–39
Blue crab
Chesapeake Bay, 116

Cottonmouth moccasin
Back Bay National Wildlife
Refuge, 110
Lake Drummond, 130–131
Cow knob salamander
Reddish Knob, 40
Ponies
Chincoteague National
Wildlife Refuge, 124
Grayson Highlands State
Park, 41–45
River otter, 175
Sea turtles
Chesapeake Bay, 115
Sika
Chincoteague National
Wildlife Refuge,
122–127
Snowshoe hare
Laurel Fork, 38–39
Whales
Chesapeake Bay, 119
White-tailed deer, 8

ZOOS
Mill Mountain Zoo,
Roanoke, 14
Virginia Zoological Park,
165–167

Other titles in the Natural Wonders/Green Guides series:

Natural Wonders of Alaska
Natural Wonders of Florida
Green Guide to Hawaii
Natural Wonders of Idaho
Natural Wonders of Maine
Natural Wonders of Massachusetts
Natural Wonders of New Hampshire
Natural Wonders of New Jersey
Natural Wonders of Ohio
Green Guide to Oregon
Natural Wonders of Southern California
Natural Wonders of Virginia
Green Guide to Washington

All books are $9.95 at bookstores.
Or order directly from the publisher (add $3.00 shipping and
handling for direct orders):

Country Roads Press
P.O. Box 286
Castine, Maine 04421
Toll-free phone number: **800-729-9179**